UBU
ROI

UBU ROI

DRAMA IN 5 ACTS by ALFRED JARRY translated from the French by Barbara Wright with 2 portraits of the author by L. Lantier and F. A. Cazals and several drawings by Jarry and Pierre Bonnard and 204 drawings by Franciszka Themerson doodled on lithographic plates All followed by

THE SONG OF THE DISEMBRAINING

and concluding with two essays on the theatre by the same author and the same translator.

A NEW DIRECTIONS BOOK

First published as New Directions Paperbook No. 105, 1961

Manufactured in the United States of America
New Directions Books are printed on acid-free paper

Published simultaneously in Canada by
Penguin Books Canada Limited
New Directions Books are published for James Laughlin
by New Directions Publishing Corporation
80 Eighth Avenue, New York 10011

TWENTY-SECOND PRINTING

This book, this play, this drama...

Jarry was not very definite in his description of *Ubu Roi*. André Gide called it 'the most extraordinary thing seen in the Theatre for a long time'. Sacha Guitry went further: 'The question whether or not it is a masterpiece seems to me idle. I believe it is a masterpiece of its kind. You will ask, what is its kind? That is very difficult to define, for it is neither strictly humour nor strictly parody. It is not related to any other form of literature... If I were forced to classify this phenomenon I should put it first among excessive caricatures, ranking it with the most original and powerful burlesques of all time.'

Since its publication and production in 1896, *Ubu Roi* has always been subjected to exalted claims or exaggerated scorn. What it really is becomes more apparent if one considers what its author really was.

Alfred Jarry was born in 1873, the son of petit bourgeois parents, in Laval, Mayenne. He was a brilliant and original boy, independent, curious, eager to live; obstinate, fierce, sarcastic, shy. In 1883 he entered the Lycée at Rennes where he learnt with extraordinary ease but would take orders from no one. He worked when he liked and not otherwise, he was a superb wrecker of classes when he felt inclined; he applied himself to sabotage with wit and intelligence. One of his professors was a M. Hébert, already known to previous generations of pupils as le Père Ébé, or P.H. Le Père Ébé was physically grotesque, flabby and piglike, lacked all dignity and authority, and had been the butt of schoolboy humour for years before Jarry's arrival at Rennes. To Jarry he became the symbol of all the ugliness and mediocrity he already saw in the world, and he became the fiercest and most bitter protagonist in the anti-Hébert ranks. He, and other schoolboys, wrote *Les Polonais*, and performed it in 1888 in a marionette theatre in the house of one of the Lycéens. This was the prototype of *Ubu Roi*.

In 1891 Jarry went to Paris where he studied under Bergson. He published *Haldernablou*, a kind of dramatic divertissement in verse and prose, he founded two reviews, wrote various works, and in 1896 he published *Ubu*. 'He had kept *Les Polonais*, he made use of it, not without altering it, completing it, adapting it. And if this text—and he made no secret of it—were not entirely his . . . it belonged to him all the more because of the importance he attached to it, because of what he saw in it and added to it.'[1]

This touches the crux of the great Ubu controversy which arose years after Jarry's death. One side claimed that Jarry had nothing to do with the original text of *Ubu Roi*, that it was written by a fellow pupil, Charles Morin, a few years before Jarry went to Rennes, and that it was merely one of a series of plays in the anti-Hébert tradition. When asked why he had not claimed the paternity of *Ubu Roi* during Jarry's lifetime, M. Morin is supposed to have answered: 'C'est qu'il n'y a pas de quoi être fier quand on a fait une connerie pareille.' But Jarry's friends were categorical that though he enjoyed mystifying, hoaxing and fooling people, there was no doubt that he was the author of *Ubu Roi*.

In any case, Jarry succeeded in interesting Lugné-Poe in the play, and in December 1896 it was staged at the Théâtre de l'Oeuvre with Gémier in the title role. It caused an uproar, was violently booed and violently applauded; it was compared with the work of Shakespeare and Rabelais, or dismissed as insipid nonsense; it was called the inspiration of modern youth, or dismissed as a rather poor joke. It was not unique in providing an outlet for spurious emotions which, funda-

mentally, never have any precise connection with the occasion that arouses them. A royal wedding does just as well, though perhaps for a different public. But the result was that after the performance Jarry, at 23, had become famous.

Monsieur Ubu

He had always been haunted by the figure of Père Ubu; it symbolised 'the cause of all his sorrows and all his revolts'. He had already included long scenes from *Ubu* in his fragmentary works, *Minutes de Sable Mémorial*, and *César-Antéchrist*. But now he became possessed by his creation and began the 'absorbing Ubique career which, dispossessing him of his own personality, was to deprive him during his lifetime of the estimation of those responsible people who, after his death, were to claim so much affection for him'.[2] He adopted a

VI

peculiar way of speaking, referred to himself always as le Père Ubu, using the regal 'we'.

It is difficult to see anything in common between the real Alfred Jarry and the es-

Alfred Jarry at the time he wrote *Ubu Roi*

sential Père Ubu. Ubu was conceived as hideous, grotesque, with a pear-shaped head, practically no hair and an enormous, flabby stomach; the embodiment of cupidity, stupidity, brutality, ferocity. Jarry, in 1903, four years before his death, was described by André Salmon as having long, dark hair falling almost to his shoulders, a face of a pure oval shape, a straight mouth, a short, well-modelled nose and black eyes that were honest and ardent. He was stubborn, shy, arrogant, incredibly proud, a rebel who liked to show off but was funda-

mentally mild and good-tempered. He loved the country, exercising, bicycling, fishing, and had a reputation for being able to catch fish where there were none.

Yet, after his metamorphosis into Ubu, he was described by Gide as 'a strange kind of clown, with a befloured face, a black beady eye and hair plastered down on his head like a skull-cap'.[3] He made himself look like a clown, and he acted the clown, in his writing and in his life. He had become a cult, others started to speak and act in a manner they imagined to be Ubuesque (but none so efficiently as Jarry); he had insinuated himself into people's imaginations, had become an avant-garde Donald Duck. 'At the Mercure (at that time)' writes André Gide, in the commemorative number of the *Mercure de France* of December, 1946, the first number to appear after the war, 'he exercised a curious kind of fascination. Everyone, almost everyone around him, attempted, with greater or lesser success, to imitate, to adopt, his style, and above all his eccentric way of speaking which was relentless, without inflection or nuance, with an equal accentuation on all syllables, even on the mutes. There would not have been the slightest difference if a nutcracker had spoken. He asserted himself without embarrassment and with a perfect disdain of convention. The surrealists, later, never invented anything better, and it is with justice that they recognise and salute in him a precursor.' Jarry's dispossession is so striking that it is a little surprising that he has not yet been elevated into the prototype of a Jarry-complex. One of his strongest impulses seems to have been the 'disgust, the fierce contempt and the icy gaiety which both people and things inspired in him'. He neither wished nor was able to adapt himself to the world as it was. He ignored the conventions of life, and even the conditions of life. He refused to compromise with something for which he felt nothing but scorn, and he accepted with indifference the logical consequence of his attitude—that life should destroy him, and much sooner than most.

Alfred Jarry in 1906, by F.-A. Cazals

When his parents died he immediately lost on one of his reviews the money they left him. After that he lived in almost perpetual poverty, refusing most of the help his friends offered. When he had no money to buy food, he drank. André Breton claimed Jarry as an absinthe-surrealist. Chauveau puts it that alcohol for Jarry was 'more than a habit, a vice or a weakness, it was a conviction, a need, a sure way of attaining the absolute. At first Jarry drank in order to scandalise, continued for the sake of continuing, then out of necessity, despair, pride and genius'.

From alcohol he went on to ether. He lived in a picturesquely filthy room on a floor called the second-and-a-half; the ceiling had been lowered and the room was a sort of cupboard between the second and third floors. He lived with two owls, (originally alive, later stuffed), a guitar, stinking flowers, masses of dirty papers, a stone phallus. Jarry's personal décor sounds familiar. He was certainly different from the bourgeois, but perhaps not so different from those who differ from the bourgeois. But his brilliance and wit were uncommon. Giving a lecture on art and artists he spoke of everything from Turkestan to Bergson, from Fragonard to angling. Afterwards one of his friends told him that he had found it very interesting but hadn't understood a word of it. Jarry answered: 'That's exactly what I wanted. Talking about things that are understandable only weighs down the mind and falsifies the memory, but the absurd exercises the mind and makes the memory work.' There are many Jarry legends. He is reputed to have been the discoverer of the Douanier Rousseau and to have introduced him to the French public as a great painter, though he personally had no belief in Rousseau's talent. Then, though he would appear in the street in a fur tiara, bedroom slippers, an overcoat falling to pieces, and armed with a loaded stick and a couple of revolvers, there is a story that when a Belgian girl who had heard him lecture, went to Paris and got herself invited to a lunch he was to attend, expecting all possible excesses, Jarry, forewarned, appeared in an impeccable black suit and behaved like the most perfectly respectable gentleman.

He spent days on end alone in his squalid room. His friends deplored his wasted talents and helped him as much as he would let them, though he would accept nothing that he thought was offered out of pity. Then for two days no one saw him. Two of his friends went to see what had become of him and found him lying on his straw bed in a state of indescribable filth, paralysed in both legs and unaware of what had happened. He was taken to hospital where he became rapidly weaker, and on the 1st November, 1907, he died, at the age of 34. His last request was for a toothpick.

Perhaps the wisest comment on him was made by Gabriel Brunet: 'Jarry's life seems to have been directed by a philosophical concept. He offered himself as a victim to the derision and to the absurdity of the world. His life is a sort of humorous and ironic epic which is carried to the point of the voluntary, farcical and thorough destruction of the self. Jarry's teaching could be summarised thus: every man is capable of showing his contempt for the cruelty and stupidity of the universe by making his own life a poem of incoherence and absurdity.'

Jarry's collected works consist of some 2,000 pages of plays, prose and poems. For a time he also wrote theatre criticisms which were brief and amusing. And his ideas on production were still considered innovations when practised much later, as for instance, by Cocteau. He wrote to Lugné-Poe in 1896:

True portrait of Monsieur Ubu

'It would be interesting . . . to be able to stage (*Ubu Roi*) . . . on the following lines:

1 Mask for the chief character, Ubu . . .

2 A cardboard horse's head which he would hang from his neck, as they did in the old English Theatre, for the only two equestrian scenes, all of whose details are in the spirit of the play, as I intended to make it a "guignol".

3 Adoption of a single set, or rather of a plain backcloth, doing away with the raising and lowering of the curtain during the single act. A conventionally dressed character would appear, as in the Guignols, and hang up a placard informing the audience of the location of the scene. (Note that I am certain that the written placard is much more "suggestive" than scenery. Neither scenery nor supers could represent "The Polish Army marching in the Ukraine".)

4 No crowds; these are a mistake on the stage and hamper the intelligence. Thus a single soldier in the Review scene, a single one in the scrimmage where Ubu says: "What a gang, what a retreat", etc.

5 The adoption of an "accent", or rather, a special "voice" for the chief character.

6 The costumes should give as little as possible the impression of local colour or chronology (this renders better the idea of something eternal). They should preferably be modern, as the satire is modern; and sordid, to make the play appear more wretched and horrific.'

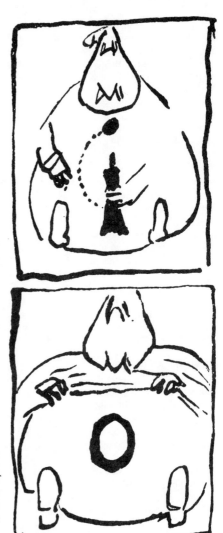

The influence of Jarry and of *Ubu Roi* has been felt in all the arts. Amédée Ozenfant[4] wrote: 'One aspect of modern poetry is often a highly emphasised extremism. That must be attributed largely to the influence of the extraordinary Jarry, the Cambronne of poetry. Jarry is the last highpowered romantic. . . . The wit, often piercing, often profound, of this professional toper, because of its monumental indifference, made an immense impression on the often highly intelligent originators of Fauvism, Cubism and Dadaism in painting, literature and music. Many contemporaries reveal this influence, most curiously allied with the eccentricities of various original characters out of Gide. Picasso, Satie, the Cocteau of *Parade* (1917), and the Apollinaire of *Les Mamelles de Tirésias* (1917), owe a debt to *Ubu Roi*.' And Apollinaire[5] '. . . those who study the literary history of our time will be amazed that, like the alchemists, the dreamers and poets devoted themselves, without even the pretext of a philosopher's stone, to inquiries and to notations which exposed them to the ridicule of their contemporaries, of journalists and of snobs.

'But their inquiries will be useful; they will be the foundation of a new realism which will perhaps not be inferior to that so poetic and learned realism of ancient Greece.

'With Alfred Jarry, moreover, we have seen laughter rise from the lower regions where it was writhing, to furnish the poet with a totally new lyricism. Where is the time when Desdemona's handkerchief seemed to be an inadmissible ridiculousness? Today even ridicule is sought after, it must be seized upon and it has its place in poetry because it is a part of life in the same way as heroism and all that formerly nourished a poet's enthusiasm.'

'As for the action, that takes place in Poland, that is to say, nowhere,'—so Jarry finished his speech introducing the first performance of *Ubu*.[6] 'The idea of something eternal,' he wrote to Lugné-Poe. Perhaps *Ubu* is eternal; it has not dated in the half-century it has been in existence. One imagines it is even more topical today than in 1896. It is timeless, placeless, it shamelessly displays what civilisation tries hard to hide, and that is more than lavatory brushes and schoolboy swearwords, it is an aspect of truth.

Barbara Wright.

1   Paul Chauveau. *Alfred Jarry, ou la Naissance, la Vie et la Mort du Père Ubu.*
2   Paul Chauveau. *Alfred Jarry, ou la Naissance, la Vie et la Mort du Père Ubu.*
3   *The Counterfeiters.* Pub. A. A. Knopf. Trans. Dorothy Bussy.

4   A. Ozenfant. *Foundations of Modern Art.* Pub. John Rodker. Trans. E. Allen Asburn.
5   G. Apollinaire. *L'Esprit Nouveau et les Poètes.* Harvill Press. Trans. R. Shattuck.
6   In 1896, when Poland's name was erased from the map.

UBU ROI

Composition of the **Orchestra**

Oboe
    Pipes
        Saveloy
   Big Bass
Flageolets   Transverse Flutes
   Concert Flute
Little Bassoon   Big Bassoon
Triple Bassoon   Little black Cornets
   Shrill white Cornets
Horns   Sackbuts   Trombones
Green Hunting-Horns   Fipple-Flutes
   Bagpipes
   Bombardons   Kettle-drums
   Drum   Bass-drum
   Grand Organs

Characters

Père Ubu
Mère Ubu
Captain Bordure
King Venceslas
Queen Rosemonde
Boleslas ⎫
Ladislas ⎬ their sons
Bougrelas ⎭
General Lascy
Stanislas Leczinski
Jean Sobieski
Nicolas Rensky
The Emperor Alexis
Giron ⎫
Pile ⎬ Palotins
Cotice ⎭
Conspirators and Soldiers

Crowd
Michel Fédérovitch
Nobles
Magistrates
Counsellors
Financiers
Financial Lacqueys
Peasants
The Whole Russian Army
The Whole Polish Army
Mère Ubu's Guards
A Captain
The Bear
The Phynancial Horse
The Disembraining Machine
The Crew
The Captain of the Ship

Then Père Ubu shakes his peare which is afterwards called Shakespeare by the Englishe and you have many excellent tragedies writen by his hand under this name.

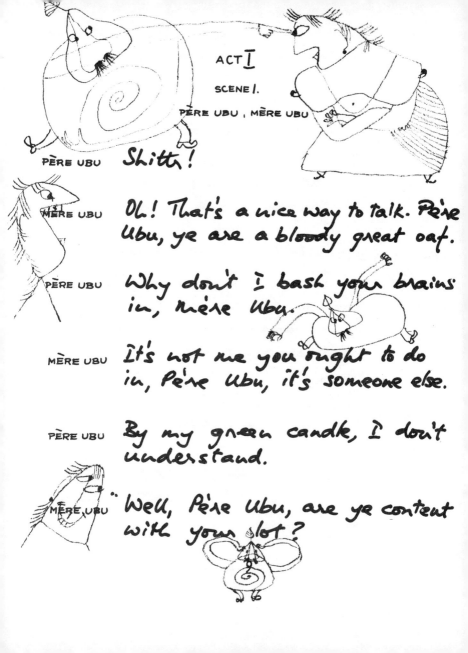

ACT I

SCENE 1.

PÈRE UBU, MÈRE UBU

PÈRE UBU   Shitt!

MÈRE UBU   Oh! That's a nice way to talk. Père Ubu, ye are a bloody great oaf.

PÈRE UBU   Why don't I bash your brains in, Mère Ubu.

MÈRE UBU   It's not me you ought to do in, Père Ubu, it's someone else.

PÈRE UBU   By my green candle, I don't understand.

MÈRE UBU   "Well, Père Ubu, are ye content with your lot?

PÈRE UBU

By my green candle, shittr, Madame, certainly I am content. I could be content with less; I'm a captain of dragoons, I'm King Wenceslas' confidential officer, I've been decorated with the Order of the Red Eagle of Poland, I'm ex-King of Aragon; what more do you want?

MÈRE UBU

What! When you've been King of Aragon, you're satisfied to lead to the Reviews a paltry fifty flunkeys armed with nothing but cabbage-cutters — when you could make the crown of Poland succeed the crown of Aragon on your noddle?

PÈRE UBU

Mm? Mère Ubu, I don't understand a word of what you're saying.

10

MÈRE UBU   How stupid you are!

PÈRE UBU   By my green candle, King Venceslas is still very much alive; and even supposing he dies, hasn't he got hordes of children?

MÈRE UBU   Who's stopping you from slaughtering the whole family and putting yourself in their place?

PÈRE UBU   Oh! Mère Ubu, you insult me, and you'll find yourself in the stewpan in a minute.

MÈRE UBU   Huh! you poor fish, if I found myself in the stewpan, who'd mend the seats of your breeches?

PÈRE UBU   Well, what of it? Isn't my arse the same as anyone else's?

MÈRE UBU If I were you, what I'd want to do with my arse would be to install it on a throne. You could increase your fortune indefinitely, have sausages whenever you liked, and ride through the streets in a carriage.

PÈRE UBU If I were King, I'd have a big headpiece made like the one I had in Aragon which those louts of Spaniards stole from me in such a shameless manner.

MÈRE UBU And you could get yourself an umbrella and a great big cloak that would come right down to your feet.

PÈRE UBU Ah! I yield to temptation. Clod of a shitr, shitr of a clod, if

12

ever I meet him on a dark
night he'll go through a bad
quarter of an hour.

MÈRE UBU   Oh good, Père Ubu, now you're
            a real man.

PÈRE UBU   Oh no, though! I, a captain
            of dragoons, slay the King of
            Poland! I'd rather die.

MÈRE UBU (ASIDE) Oh shitt! (ALOUD) Then are you
            going to stay as poor as a
            rat, Père Ubu?

PÈRE UBU   Gadzookers, by my green candle,
            I prefer to be as poor as a
            skinny, honest rat than as
            rich as a vicious, fat cat.

MÈRE UBU   And the cape? and the umbrella?

and the great big cloak?

PÈRE UBU And what of them, Mère Ubu?
(HE GOES OFF BANGING THE DOOR)

MÈRE UBU Fart, shitr, it's hard to get him moving, but fart, shitr, I reckon I've shaken him all the same. Thanks to God and myself, in a week, maybe, I'll be Queen of Poland.

SCENE 2.

THE SCENE REPRESENTS A ROOM IN PÈRE UBU'S HOUSE, WHERE A MAGNIFICENT MEAL IS PREPARED.

PÈRE UBU, MÈRE UBU

MÈRE UBU Huh! our guests are extremely late.

PÈRE UBU Yes, by my green candle. I'm starving. Mère Ubu, you're exceedingly ugly today. Is it because we have visitors?

MÈRE UBU (SHRUGGING HER SHOULDERS) Shitts!

PÈRE UBU (SEIZING A ROAST CHICKEN) Look here, I'm hungry, I'm going to take a bite of this bird. It's a chicken I believe. It's not bad.

MÈRE UBU What are you doing, you ass? What will our guests have to eat?

PÈRE UBU Oh, there'll be enough for them. I won't touch anything else. Mère Ubu, go over to the window and see if our guests are coming.

MÈRE UBU (GOING OVER)

I can't see anything.

(IN THE MEANTIME PÈRE UBU PINCHES A FILLET OF VEAL)

MÈRE UBU   Ah! here comes Captain Bordure with his partisans. But what are you eating, Père Ubu?

PÈRE UBU   Nothing, a bit of veal.

MÈRE UBU   Oh the veal, the veal, vile creature! He's eaten the veal! Help!

PÈRE UBU   By my green candle, I'll tear your eyes out.

(THE DOOR OPENS)

16

SCENE 3.

PÈRE UBU, MÈRE UBU, CAPTAIN BORDURE AND HIS PARTISANS.

MÈRE UBU   Good day, gentlemen, we were awaiting you impatiently. Sit down.

CAPT.BORDURE   Good day, Madame. But where on earth is Père Ubu?

PÈRE UBU   Here I am! here I am! Damn it, by my green candle, I'm fat enough, I should have thought.

CAPT.BORDURE   Good day, Père Ubu. Sit down, my men.

(THEY ALL SIT DOWN)

PÈRE UBU   Phew! a bit more and I'd have stove in my chair.

17

CAPT. BORDURE: Well, mère Ubu, what are you giving us today that's good?

MÈRE UBU: Here's the menu.

PÈRE UBU: Oh, I'm interested in that.

MÈRE UBU: Soupe polonaise, rastron ribs, veal, chicken, dog pie, turkeys' rumps, charlotte russe.

PÈRE UBU: Hey, that's enough, I should think. Is there any more?

MÈRE UBU: (CONTINUING) Ice pudding, salad, fruit, dessert, boiled beef, jerusalem artichokes, cauliflower à la shittr.

PÈRE UBU: Huh! do you think I'm the Emperor of Orient that you spend such a lot?

MÈRE UBU Don't listen to him, he's an imbecile.

PÈRE UBU Ah! I'll sharpen my teeth on your calves.

MÈRE UBU Have your dinner instead, Père Ubu. Here's some polonaise.

PÈRE UBU Hell, it's awful.

CAPT. BORDURE It's certainly not very nice.

MÈRE UBU Bunch of crooks, what do you want, then?

PÈRE UBU (STRIKING HIS FOREHEAD) Oh, I've got an idea. I'll be back in a minute. (HE GOES OFF)

MÈRE UBU Gentlemen, let's try some veal.

19

CAPT. BORDURE It's very good, I've finished.

MÈRE UBU Now for the rumps.

CAPT. BORDURE Exquisite, exquisite! Long live Mère Ubu.

ALL Long live Mère Ubu.

PÈRE UBU (COMING BACK) And you'll soon be saying long live Père Ubu.

(HE HAS A LAVATORY BRUSH IN HIS HAND AND THROWS IT ON TO THE FESTIVE BOARD)

MÈRE UBU Blockhead, what are you doing?

PÈRE UBU Taste it.

(SEVERAL TASTE IT AND ARE POISONED)

20

PÈRE UBU Mère Ubu, pass me the rashon cutlets so that I can serve them.

MÈRE UBU Here you are.

PÈRE UBU Outside, everyone! Captain Bordure, I want to talk to you.

THE OTHERS Hey, we haven't had anything to eat.

PÈRE UBU What d'you mean, you haven't had anything to eat? Out you go, everybody. Stay here, Bordure.

(NO ONE BUDGES)

PÈRE UBU Haven't you gone yet? By my green candle, I'll do you in with rastron ribs.

(HE BEGINS TO THROW THEM)

ALL Oo! Ouch! Help! Defend yourselves! Murder! I'm dead!

PÈRE UBU Shittr, shittr, shittr! Outside! I'm cleverer than I thought!

ALL Every man for himself! Lousy Père Ubu! Traitor and mean skunk!

PÈRE UBU Ah! they've gone. I can breathe, but I've had a rotten dinner. Come on, Bordure.

(THEY GO OUT WITH MÈRE UBU)

22

MÈRE UBU, PÈRE UBU, CAPTAIN BORDURE.

PÈRE UBU   Well, Captain, did you have a good dinner?

CAPT. BORDURE   Very good, Monsieur, except for the shitts.

PÈRE UBU   Huh! the shitts wasn't bad.

MÈRE UBU   There's no accounting for tastes.

PÈRE UBU   Captain Bordure, I've decided to make you Duke of Lithuania.

CAPT. BORDURE   What? I thought you were very badly off, Père Ubu.

PÈRE UBU   In a few days, if you choose, I shall reign over Poland.

CAPT. BORDURE Are you going to kill Venceslas?

PÈRE UBU This fellow's no fool, he's guessed.

CAPT. BORDURE If it's a question of killing Venceslas, I'm on. I'm his mortal enemy, and I'll answer for my men.

PÈRE UBU (THROWING HIMSELF ON HIM AND KISSING HIM)

Oh, oh, I'm very fond of you, Bordure.

CAPT. BORDURE Pooh, you stink, Père Ubu. Don't you ever wash?

24

PÈRE UBU   Sometimes.

MÈRE UBU   Never!

PÈRE UBU   I'll tread on your toes.

MÈRE UBU   Big shitts!

PÈRE UBU   Well, Bordure, I've done with you. But, by my green candle, I swear by mère ubu to make you Duke of Lithuania.

MÈRE UBU   But...

PÈRE UBU   Be quiet, my sweet child.

(THEY GO OUT)

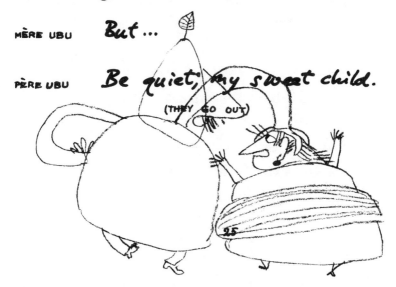

25

SCENE 5.

PÈRE UBU, MÈRE UBU, A MESSENGER.

PÈRE UBU Monsieur, what do you want? Go away, you bore me.

MESSENGER Monsieur, you are summoned to the King's presence.

PÈRE UBU Oh shittr! gadzookers! by my green candle, I am discovered! I'll lose my head! Alas! Alack!

MÈRE UBU What a feeble man! And there's not much time.

PÈRE UBU Ah! I've got an idea. I'll say that it was Mère Ubu and Bordure.

MÈRE UBU   Oh! Fat P.U., if you do that...

PÈRE UBU   Mrr! I'll go this minute.
                     (HE GOES OUT)

MÈRE UBU (RUNNING AFTER HIM) Hi! Père Ubu, Père Ubu, I'll give you some grub.
                     (SHE GOES OUT)

PÈRE UBU (OFF) Oh! Shittr! You're a grub yourself.

SCENE 6.

KING VENCESLAS, SURROUNDED BY HIS OFFICERS; BORDURE;

THE KING'S SONS: BOLESLAS, LADISLAS, BOUGRELAS; THEN

PÈRE UBU

PÈRE UBU (ENTERING) Oh! you know, it wasn't me, it was Mère Ubu and Bordure.

THE KING   What's the matter, Père Ubu?

27

CAPT. BORDURE He's had too much to drink.

THE KING Like me this morning.

PÈRE UBU Yes, I'm boozed, it's because I've drunk too much French wine.

THE KING Père Ubu, I want to recognise your numerous services as Captain of Dragoons, and I am making you Count of Sandomir as from today.

28

PÈRE UBU Oh Monsieur Venceslas, I don't know how to thank you.

THE KING Don't thank me, Père Ubu, and be present tomorrow morning at the great review.

PÈRE UBU I'll be there, but be good enough to accept this little toy whistle.

(HE PRESENTS THE KING WITH A TOY WHISTLE.)

THE KING What do you expect me to do with a toy whistle at my age? I'll give it to Bougrelas.

BOUGRELAS What an ass that Père Ubu is.

PÈRE UBU Now I'll bugger off.

(AS HE TURNS ROUND HE FALLS DOWN)

29

Oh! Ow! Help! By my green candle, I've ruptured my intestine and busted my dungzine.

THE KING (PICKING HIM UP) Père Ubu, hast hurt thyself?

PÈRE UBU Yes indeed I have, and I shall certainly pass away. What will happen to Mère Ubu?

THE KING We shall provide for her

PÈRE UBU Your kindness knows no bounds. (HE GOES OUT) Yes but, King Venceslas, you won't be any the less slaughtered, you know.

30

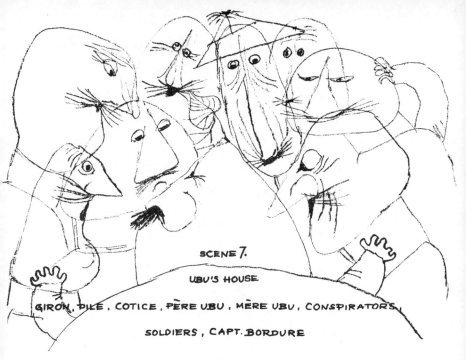

SCENE 7.

UBU'S HOUSE

GIRON, PILE, COTICE, PÈRE UBU, MÈRE UBU, CONSPIRATORS,
SOLDIERS, CAPT. BORDURE

PÈRE UBU   Well, my good friends, it's high
time to decide on our plans for
the conspiracy. Let's hear
everybody's views. First of
all I'll tell you mine, if you'll
allow me.

CAPT. BORDURE   Go ahead, Père Ubu.

31:

PÈRE UBU   Well then, my friends, in my opinion we should simply poison the King by sticking some arsenic in his lunch. When he starts stuffing himself he'll fall down dead, and then I'll be King.

ALL   Pooh, what a lousy beast.

PÈRE UBU   So what? Doesn't that suit you? Then let Bordure say what he thinks.

CAPT. BORDURE   I think we should give him a terrific blow with a sword and split him open from head to middle.

ALL   Yes, that's noble and gallant.

PÈRE UBU   And what if he starts kicking you? I remember now that when there's a review on he wears iron shoes that hurt very badly. If I had any sense i'd go off and denounce you to get myself out of this dirty business, and I reckon he'd give me some cash, as well.

MÈRE UBU   Oh the traitor, the coward, the villain and mean skunk.

ALL   Down with Père Ub!

PÈRE UBU   Hey, gentlemen, keep quiet if you don't want to be put in my pocket. Anyway, I agree to expose myself for you. So you, Bordure, make yourself

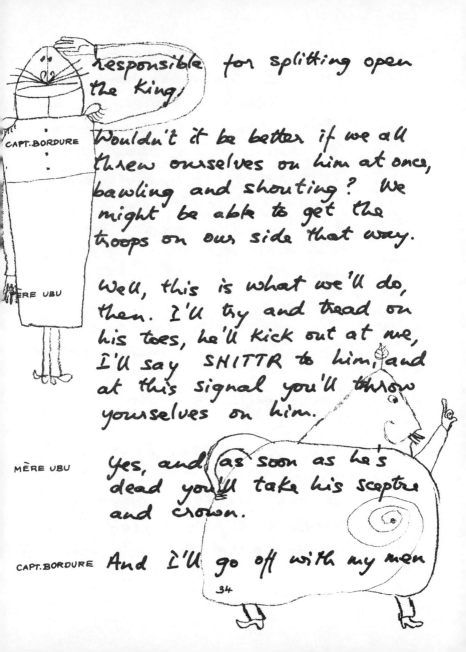

responsible for splitting open the King.

CAPT. BORDURE Wouldn't it be better if we all threw ourselves on him at once, bawling and shouting? We might be able to get the troops on our side that way.

PÈRE UBU Well, this is what we'll do, then. I'll try and tread on his toes, he'll kick out at me, I'll say SHITTR to him, and at this signal you'll throw yourselves on him.

MÈRE UBU Yes, and as soon as he's dead you'll take his sceptre and crown.

CAPT. BORDURE And I'll go off with my men

34

in pursuit of the royal family.

PÈRE UBU   Yes, and I specially recommend young Bougrelas to you.

(THEY GO OUT)

PÈRE UBU (RUNNING AFTER THEM AND MAKING THEM COME BACK)

Gentlemen, we have forgotten an indispensable ceremony; we must swear to fight gallantly.

CAPT. BORDURE   But how can we? We haven't got a priest.

PÈRE UBU   Mère Ubu will stand in for one.

ALL   All right, so be it!

PÈRE UBU   Then you swear to kill the King properly?

ALL   Yes, we swear. Long live Père Ubu!

35

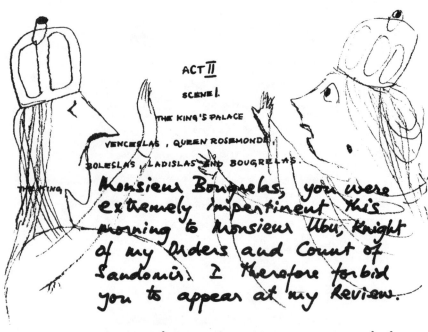

ACT II

SCENE 1.

THE KING'S PALACE

VENCESLAS, QUEEN ROSEMONDE,

BOLESLAS, LADISLAS AND BOUGRELAS.

THE KING Monsieur Bougrelas, you were extremely impertinent this morning to Monsieur Ubu, Knight of my Orders and Count of Sandomir. I therefore forbid you to appear at my Review.

THE QUEEN But Venceslas, even your whole family would not be overmany to defend you.

THE KING Madame, I never go back on my word. You weary me with your idle chatter.

36

YOUNG BOUGRELAS   I defer to your wishes, Lord and Father.

THE QUEEN   Have you decided after all, Sire, to go to this Review?

THE KING   And why shouldn't I, Madame?

THE QUEEN   But once again, haven't I seen him in a dream, smiting you with the force of his arms and throwing you into the Vistula, and an eagle, like the one in the Arms of Poland, placing the crown on his head?

THE KING   Whose head?

THE QUEEN   Père Ubu's.

THE KING   What nonsense. Monsieur de Ubu is a most upright gentleman who would allow himself to be drawn and quartered to serve me.

THE Q. & BOUGR.   What a delusion!

THE KING   Be quiet, you young lout. And you, Madame, to prove to you how little I fear Monsieur Ubu, I shall go to the Review as I am, unarmed and without a sword.

THE QUEEN   Fatal imprudence, I shall never see you alive again.

THE KING   Come, Ladislas, come, Boleslas.

(THEY GO OUT THE QUEEN AND BOUGRELAS GO TO THE WINDOW)

38

THE Q. & BOUGR. God and the great Saint Nicholas keep you!

THE QUEEN Bougrelas, come into the chapel with me to pray for your father and your brothers.

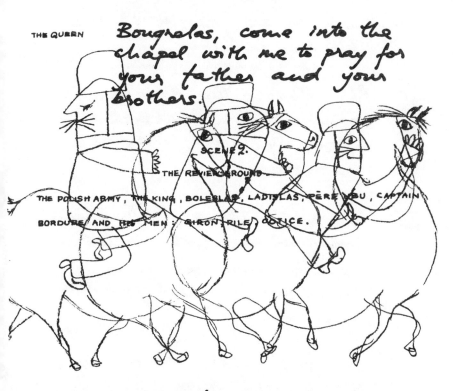

SCENE 2.
THE REVIEW GROUND
THE POLISH ARMY, THE KING, BOLESLAS, LADISLAS, PÈRE UBU, CAPTAIN BORDURE AND HIS MEN; GIRON, PILE, COTICE.

THE KING Noble Père Ubu, bring your attendants, and take your

39

place near me for the inspection of the troops.

PÈRE UBU (TO HIS MEN) Be ready, you fellows. (TO THE KING) We are coming.

(UBU'S MEN SURROUND THE KING)

THE KING Ah! There's the Horseguards regiment from Dantzick. Upon my word, they are magnificent.

PÈRE UBU Do you think so? They look lousy to me. Look at that one. (TO THE SOLDIER) How long is it since you washed your face, vile knave?

THE KING But this soldier is very clean. What's the matter with you, Père Ubu?

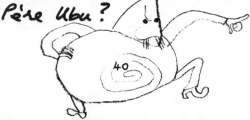

PÈRE UBU This ! (HE STAMPS ON HIS FOOT)

THE KING Wretch !

PÈRE UBU Shittr ! Come on, men !

CAPT. BORDURE Hurrah ! Advance !

(ALL STRIKE THE KING ; A PALOTIN EXPLODES)

THE KING Oh ! Help ! Holy Virgin, I'm dead.

BOLESLAS (TO LADISLAS) What's happening ?

PÈRE UBU Ah ! I've got the crown. After the others, now.

CAPT. BORDURE At the traitors !!

(THE KING'S SONS FLEE ; ALL PURSUE THEM.)

SCENE 3.

THE QUEEN AND BOUGRELAS

THE QUEEN At last I'm beginning to feel reassured.

BOUGRELAS You have nothing to fear.

(A FRIGHTFUL DIN IS HEARD OUTSIDE)

Oh! What do I see? My two brothers pursued by Père Ubu and his men.

THE QUEEN Oh God! Holy Virgin, they're losing, they're losing ground.

BOUGRELAS The whole army is following Père Ubu. The King is no longer there. Horrors! Help!

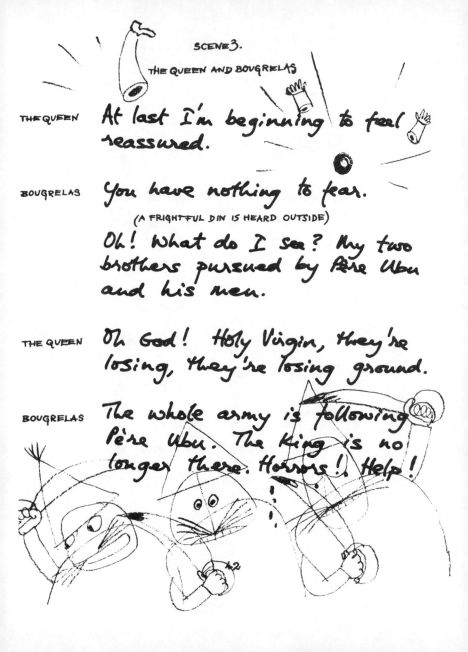

THE QUEEN Boleslas is dead! He's been hit by a bullet.

BOUGRELAS Hey! Ladislas! Defend yourself! Hurrah, Ladislas!

THE QUEEN Oh! he's surrounded.

BOUGRELAS He's breathed his last. Bordure has cut him in two like a sausage.

THE QUEEN Oh! Alas! Those madmen have got into the palace; they're coming up the stairs.

(THE NOISE INCREASES)

THE Q. AND B. (ON THEIR KNEES) Oh, God, defend us!

BOUGRELAS Oh! That Père Ubu. The villain, the wretch, if I had hold of him...

THE SAME. THE DOOR IS BROKEN DOWN. PÈRE UBU AND HIS MADMEN ENTER.

PÈRE UBU   Well, Bougrelas, what do you
                want to do to me?

BOUGRELAS   Great God! I shall defend
                my mother to the death. The
                first to take a step is a
                dead man.

PÈRE UBU   Oh, Bordure, I'm frightened!
                Let me get out of here.

A SOLDIER (ADVANCING)   Hands up, Bougrelas.

YOUNG BOUGRELAS   Here, scum, this is for you!
                (HE SPLITS HIS SKULL)

THE QUEEN   Stand fast, Bougrelas, stand
                fast.

SEVERAL (ADVANCING) Bougrelas, we promise to spare your life.

BOUGRELAS Rogues, topers, hirelings!
(HE FLOURISHES HIS SWORD AND SLAUGHTERS THEM)

PÈRE UBU Oh! I shall prevail, just the same.

BOUGRELAS Mother, escape by the secret stairway.

THE QUEEN And you, my son, and you?

BOUGRELAS I'll follow you.

PÈRE UBU Try and catch the Queen. Ah! She's got away. As for you, my lad...
(HE ADVANCES TOWARDS BOUGRELAS)

45

BOUGRELAS Ah! Great God! This is my vengeance.

(HE RIPS OPEN PÈRE UBU'S BOODLE WITH A TERRIBLE STROKE OF HIS SWORD.)

Mother, I'm coming!

(HE DISAPPEARS BY THE SECRET STAIRWAY)

SCENE 5.

A CAVE IN THE MOUNTAINS.

YOUNG BOUGRELAS ENTERS, FOLLOWED BY ROSEMONDE.

BOUGRELAS We shall be safe here.

THE QUEEN Yes, I believe so. Bougrelas, help me. (SHE FALLS ON TO THE SNOW.)

BOUGRELAS Oh! What's the matter, mother?

THE QUEEN I am grievously ill, believe me, Bougrelas. I have no more than two hours to live.

BOUGRELAS What! Are you overcome by the cold?

THE QUEEN How can I resist so many blows? The king slain, our family destroyed, and you, a scion of the most noble race that ever carried a sword, forced to flee into the mountains like a smuggler.

BOUGRELAS And by whom, great God, by whom? A vulgar Père Ubu, an adventurer who comes no one knows from where, a vile scoundrel, a disreputable vagabond! And when I think that my father had decorated him and made him a Count, and that the next day the

villain was not ashamed
to lay hands on him...

THE QUEEN Oh Bougrelas, when I remember
how happy we were before
that Père Ubu came along.
But now, alas! everything
is altered.

BOUGRELAS It can't be helped. We must
wait and hope, and never
renounce our rights.

THE QUEEN I still hope for you, my dear
child, but as for me, I shall
never live to see that happy
day.

BOUGRELAS Oh! What's the matter? She
pales, she falls. Help! But
I am in a desert! Oh God!

56

Her heart has stopped beating.
She is dead! Is it possible?
Another victim of Père Ubu!

(HE HIDES HIS FACE IN HIS HANDS AND WEEPS)

Oh God! how sad it is to
find oneself alone at fourteen
with a terrible vengeance to
pursue.

(HE FALLS A PREY TO THE MOST VIOLENT DESPAIR)

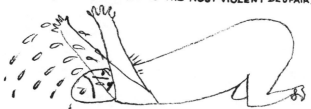

(MEANWHILE THE SOULS OF VENCESLAS, BOLESLAS AND

ROSEMONDE ENTER THE GROTTO, THEIR ANCESTORS

ACCOMPANY THEM AND FILL THE GROTTO. THE OLDEST

OF THEM APPROCHES BOUGRELAS AND GENTLY AWAKENS HIM.)

BOUGRELAS   Ah! what do I see? All my
family, my ancestors... By
what miracle?

49

THE SHADE Learn, Bougrelas, that during my lifetime I was Seigneur Mathias of Königsberg, the first King and founder of the House. I leave our vengeance in your hands. (HE GIVES HIM A LARGE SWORD) And let this sword that I give you find no rest until it shall have dealt death to the usurper.

(ALL DISAPPEAR, AND BOUGRELAS IS LEFT ALONE IN AN ATTITUDE OF EXTASY.)

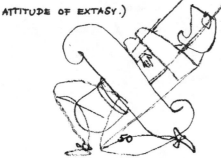

50

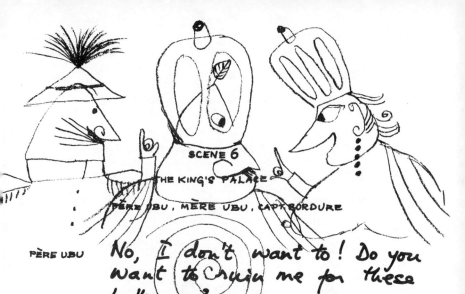

SCENE 6

THE KING'S PALACE

PÈRE UBU, MÈRE UBU, CAPT. BORDURE

PÈRE UBU   No, I don't want to! Do you want to ruin me for these buffoons?

CAPT. BORDURE   But look, Père Ubu, don't you see that the people are waiting for the gift of the joyous accession?

MÈRE UBU   If you don't distribute some meat and gold you'll be overthrown in a couple of hours.

PÈRE UBU Meat, yes! Gold, no! Slaughter three old nags, that'll be good enough for such asses.

MÈRE UBU Ass yourself! How did *I* get landed with such an animal?

PÈRE UBU Once and for all, *I* want to get rich, and *I* won't part with a sou!

MÈRE UBU When we have all the wealth of Poland at our disposal.

CAPT. BORDURE Yes, *I* know that there's a terrific hoard in the chapel; we'll distribute it.

52

PÈRE UBU Bastard! if you do that...

CAPT. BORDURE But Père Ubu, if you don't distribute anything, the people won't want to pay the taxes.

PÈRE UBU Is that really true?

MÈRE UBU Of course it is.

PÈRE UBU Oh well, then, I agree to everything. Get together three millions, cook a hundred and fifty oxen and sheep, especially as I'll have some as well!

(THEY GO OUT)

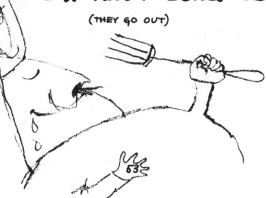

53

THE COURTYARD OF THE PALACE, FULL OF PEOPLE

PÈRE UBU, CROWNED, MÈRE UBU, CAPT. BORDURE, LACQUEYS CARRYING MEAT.

PEOPLE   Here's the King! Long live the King! Hurrah!

PÈRE UBU (THROWING GOLD) Here you are, this is for you. It didn't particularly amuse me to give you any money, but you know it was Mère Ubu who wanted to. At least promise that you'll really pay the taxes.

ALL   Yes, yes!

CAPT. BORDURE   Look, Mère Ubu, how they're fighting over the gold. What a battle!

54

MÈRE UBU It's truly horrible. Pooh! There's one with his skull split open.

PÈRE UBU What a wonderful sight! Bring some more cases of gold.

CAPT. BORDURE Let's get them to race.

PÈRE UBU Yes, that's an idea. (TO THE PEOPLE) My friends, you see this case full of gold? It contains 300,000 gold rose nobles in Polish money, and it's genuine. Those of you who want to race, go down to the end of the courtyard. Start when I wave my handkerchief, and the first to arrive will get the case. As for those who don't win, they can share

55

this other case as a consolation
prize.

ALL   Yes! Long live Père Ubu!
What a good king! We never
saw so much money in Venceslas'
time.

PÈRE UBU (JOYFULLY, TO MÈRE UBU) Listen to them!

(ALL THE PEOPLE GO AND LINE UP AT THE END OF THE COURTYARD)

One, two, three, are you ready?

ALL   Yes! Yes!

PÈRE UBU   Go!

(THEY START OFF, TRIPPING OVER EACH OTHER. CRIES AND UPROAR)

56

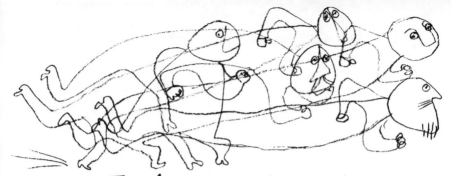

CAPT. BORDURE They're coming! They're coming!

PÈRE UBU And the one in front is losing ground.

MÈRE UBU No, he's making it up again.

CAPT BORDURE Oh! he's lost, he's lost! _It's_ over. It's the other one.

(THE ONE WHO WAS SECOND GETS IN FIRST.)

ALL Long live Michel Fédérovitch! Long live Michel Fédérovitch!

MICHEL FÉDÉROVITCH Sire, I really don't know how to thank your Majesty.

PÈRE UBU   Oh my dear friend, it's nothing. Take the case home with you, Michel, and you, share the other. Take one piece each until there aren't any left.

ALL   Long live Michel Fédérovitch! Long live Père Ubu!

PÈRE UBU   And you, my friends, come and have dinner! I throw open the doors of the palace to you, come and do justice to my table!

PEOPLE   Let's go in! Let's go in! Long live Père Ubu! He is the most noble of sovereigns.

(THEY ENTER THE PALACE. THE NOISE OF THE ORGY, WHICH GOES ON TILL THE NEXT DAY, CAN BE HEARD. THE CURTAIN FALLS.)

58

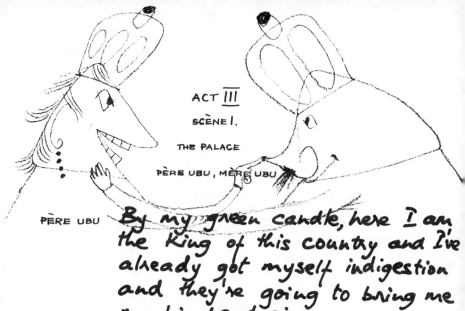

ACT III

SCÈNE I.

THE PALACE

PÈRE UBU, MÈRE UBU

PÈRE UBU By my green candle, here I am the King of this country and I've already got myself indigestion and they're going to bring me my big head piece.

MÈRE UBU What's it made of, Père Ubu?— because even if we are the Sovereigns, we must be economical.

PÈRE UBU Madame my female, it's made of sheepskin, with a clasp and tie-strings of dogskin.

59

MÈRE UBU That's wonderful, but it's even more wonderful to be King and Queen.

PÈRE UBU Yes, you were right, Mère Ubu.

MÈRE UBU We owe a big debt of gratitude to the Duke of Lithuania.

PÈRE UBU Who to?

MÈRE UBU Why, Captain Bordure.

PÈRE UBU For goodness' sake, Mère Ubu, don't speak to me about that buffoon. Now that I don't need him any more he can whistle for it, he won't get his Dukedom.

MÈRE UBU You are very wrong, Père Ubu, he'll turn against you.

60

PÈRE UBU   Oh, I'm very sorry for the little man, I worry about him as much as I do about Bougrelas.

MÈRE UBU   And do you think you've finished with Bougrelas?

PÈRE UBU   By my financial sabre, of course! What do you expect him to do to me, that little urchin of fourteen?

MÈRE UBU   Père Ubu, pay attention to what I say. Believe me, you should try to attach Bougrelas to you by your good deeds.

PÈRE UBU   Dole out more money? Not bloody likely! You've already made me waste at least twenty two millions.

61

MÈRE UBU Please yourself, Père Ubu, but you'll find yourself in the soup.

PÈRE UBU Oh well, you'll be in the soup with me.

MÈRE UBU Listen, once more, I'm sure that young Bougrelas will get the better of you because he has right on his side.

PÈRE UBU Oh tripe! Isn't it just as good to have wrong on your side as it is to have right? Pooh, you insult me, mère Ubu, I'll cut you to pieces.

(MÈRE UBU RUNS AWAY, PURSUED BY PÈRE UBU)

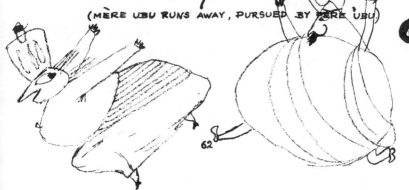

THE GREAT HALL OF THE PALACE

PÈRE UBU , MÈRE UBU , OFFICERS AND SOLDIERS ; GIRON , PILE , COTICE ;

NOBLES IN CHAINS , FINANCIERS , MAGISTRATES , CLERKS.

PÈRE UBU Bring the Nobles' coffer and the Nobles' hook and the Nobles' knife and the Nobles' book. And then bring the Nobles.

(THE NOBLES ARE BRUTALLY PUSHED IN.)

MÈRE UBU For goodness sake restrain yourself, Père Ubu.

PÈRE UBU I have the honour to announce to you that in order to enrich the Kingdom I'm going to have all the Nobles put to death and help myself to their property.

63

NOBLES   Horrors! Help, people and soldiers!

PÈRE UBU   Bring the first Noble and pass me the Nobles' hook. Those who are condemned to death will be passed down the trap door and fall into the basements of the pig-pinching machine and the cash-room where they will be disembrained. (TO THE NOBLE) Who are you, buffoon?

NOBLE   Count of Vitepsk.

PÈRE UBU   What's your income?

NOBLE   Three million rix-dollars.

PÈRE UBU   Condemned!

(HE GRABS HIM WITH THE HOOK AND PASSES HIM TO THE PIT.)

64

MÈRE UBU What beastly savagery!

PÈRE UBU Second Noble, who are you?

(THE NOBLE DOESN'T REPLY)

Are you going to answer, buffoon?

NOBLE Grand Duke of Posen.

PÈRE UBU Excellent! Excellent! That's all I want to know. Down the trap door. Third Noble, who are you? You've got an ugly mug.

NOBLE Duke of Courland, of the towns of Riga, of Revel, and of Mitau.

PÈRE UBU Good! Fine! Is that all?

NOBLE That's all.

PÈRE UBU Down the trap door, then. Fourth

Noble, who are you?

NOBLE Prince of Podolia.

PÈRE UBU What's your income?

NOBLE I am ruined.

PÈRE UBU For that ugly word- down the trap door with you. Fifth Noble, who are you?

NOBLE Margrave of Thorn, Palatine of Polock.

PÈRE UBU That's not much. Is that all?

NOBLE It was enough for me.

PÈRE UBU Oh well, a little's better than nothing. Down the trap door. What are you nattering about, Mère Ubu?

MÈRE UBU You're too bloodthirsty, Père Ubu.

PÈRE UBU Huh! I'm getting rich! I'm going to have MY list of MY property read. Clerk, read MY list of MY property.

CLERK County of Sandomir.

PÈRE UBU Begin with the princedoms, stupid ass.

CLERK Princedom of Podolia, Grand Duchy of Posen, Duchy of Courland, County of Sandomir, County of Vitepsk, Palatinate of Polock, Margraviate of Thorn.

PÈRE UBU Then what?

CLERK That's all.

PÈRE UBU   What, is that all? Oh well then, come on, Nobles, and as I intend to continue enriching myself I shall have all the Nobles executed and thus get hold of all the vacant properties. Come on, pass the Nobles through the trap door.

(THE NOBLES ARE SHOVED THROUGH THE TRAP-DOOR)

Hurry up quicker, I want to make some laws now.

SEVERAL   That'll be something.

PÈRE UBU   First I shall reform the law, after which we shall proceed to Finance.

MAGISTRATES   We are opposed to all change.

PÈRE UBU   Shitt! Firstly, magistrates won't be paid any more.

MAGISTRATES And what shall we live on? We are poor.

PÈRE UBU You can have the fines that you impose and the property of the people who are condemned to death.

A MAGISTRATE Horrors!

A SECOND Infamy!

A THIRD Shame!

A FOURTH Indignity!

ALL We object to passing judgment under such conditions.

PÈRE UBU All the Magistrates down the trap door! (THEY STRUGGLE IN VAIN)

MÈRE UBU   Here! What are you doing, Père Ubu? Who'll administer justice now?

PÈRE UBU   Huh! I shall. You'll see how well it'll work.

MÈRE UBU   Yes, that'll be a fine mess.

PÈRE UBU   Look, shut up, buffooness. And now, gentlemen, we shall proceed to Finance.

FINANCIERS   There's nothing to change.

PÈRE UBU   But I'm going to change everything. In the first place, I intend to keep half the taxes for myself.

FINANCIERS   What d'you think of that!

70

PÈRE UBU Gentlemen, we shall institute a tax of 10% on property, another on commerce and industry, and a third on marriages, and a fourth on deaths, each of fifteen francs.

FIRST FINANCIER But it's idiotic, Père Ubu.

SECOND FINANCIER It's absurd.

THIRD FINANCIER You can't make head or tail of it.

PÈRE UBU What d'you think I am? Down the trap door with the Financiers.

(THE FINANCIERS ARE PUSHED IN.)

MÈRE UBU But look here, Père Ubu, what sort of a King do you think you are, you kill everyone.

PÈRE UBU Oh shittr!

MÈRE UBU No more Law, no more Finance!

PÈRE UBU Don't be afraid, my sweet child, I'll go myself from village to village and collect the taxes.

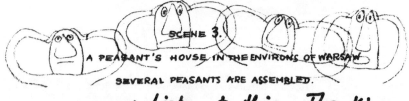

SCENE 3.

A PEASANT'S HOUSE IN THE ENVIRONS OF WARSAW

SEVERAL PEASANTS ARE ASSEMBLED.

A PEASANT (ENTERING) Listen to this. The King is dead, so are the Dukes, and young Bougrelas has fled to the mountains with his mother. What's more, Père Ubu has seized the throne.

72

ANOTHER I've heard even more than that. I've just come from Cracow where I saw them taking away the bodies of more than three hundred Nobles and five hundred Magistrates whom they'd killed, and it seems that they're going to double the taxes, and that Père Ubu will come and collect them himself.

ALL Great God! What will become of us? Père Ubu's a fearful beast and his family, they say, is abominable.

A PEASANT But listen, wouldn't you say that someone was knocking at the door?

73

A VOICE (OFF) Horngibolets! Open, by my shittr, by St. John, St. Peter and St. Nicholas! Open, sabre of finance, horns of finance! I've come to collect the taxes.

(THE DOOR IS BROKEN DOWN AND UBU COMES IN, FOLLOWED BY HORDES OF TAX-COLLECTORS.)

PÈRE UBU

SCENE 4.

Which of you is the oldest? (A PEASANT COMES FORWARD) What's your name?

THE PEASANT Stanislas Leczinski.

PÈRE UBU Well then, horngibolets! listen well, or these gentlemen will cut

off your *earens*. But are you
going to listen, at least?

STANISLAS But your Excellency hasn't
said anything yet.

PÈRE UBU What! I've been speaking for
the last hour. Do you think
I came here to preach in
the wilderness?

STANISLAS Far be it from me, such a thought.

PÈRE UBU Well, I've come to tell you, to
order you, and to intimate to
you that you are to produce
and exhibit your cash promptly,
or you'll be done in. Come on,
my Lords the Salopins of Finance,
convey here the phynancial
conveyance. (THEY BRING THE CONVEYANCE)

STANISLAS Sire, we are only down on the register for a hundred and fifty two rix-dollars, and we have already paid those six weeks ago come St. Matthew's day.

PÈRE UBU Very likely, but I've changed the government and I've had it put in the paper that all the existing taxes must be paid twice, and those that _I_ shall impose later must be paid three times. With this system I shall soon have made my fortune, then I'll kill everybody and go away.

PEASANTS Monsieur Ubu, have mercy, have pity on us, we are poor citizens.

PÈRE UBU What do I care? Pay up.

PEASANTS We can't, we've already paid.

PÈRE UBU Pay up! or into my pocket with you, with torture and decapitation of the neck and head. Horngibolets! I am the king, I suppose?

ALL Ah! So that's how it is! To arms! Long live Bougrelas, by the grace of God, king of Poland and of Lithuania.

PÈRE UBU Advance, gentlemen of Finance, do your duty.

(A STRUGGLE TAKES PLACE. THE HOUSE IS DESTROYED, AND OLD STANISLAS RUNS AWAY ALONE ACROSS THE PLAIN. UBU STAYS TO COLLECT THE MONEY.)

SCENE 5.

A DUNGEON IN THE FORTIFICATIONS OF THORN.

BORDURE, IN CHAINS. PÈRE UBU

PÈRE UBU Ah, citizen, so this is where it's got you – you wanted me to pay you what *I* owed you and you revolted because *I* didn't want to. You started a conspiracy, and here you are in jug. Horns of finance, it's worked out all right, and the trick has come off so well that you must be quite pleased with it yourself.

BORDURE Take care, Père Ubu. In the five days that you have been king you have committed more murders than it would take to damn all the Saints of Paradise. The blood of the

78

King and of the Nobles is crying, out for vengeance, and it's cries will be heard.

PÈRE UBU Ha, my fine friend, you have a glib tongue. I don't doubt that if you were to escape, quite a few complications would ensue, but I don't think the dungeons of Thorn have ever let out any of the honest fellows who have been entrusted to them. So that's why I bid you good night, and I advise you to sleep soundly, although the rats dance quite a nice saraband here.

(HE GOES OUT. THE LACQUEYS COME AND BOLT ALL THE DOORS)

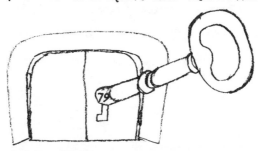

79

SCENE 6.

THE PALACE IN MOSCOW

THE EMPEROR ALEXIS AND HIS COURT, BORDURE.

THE CZAR ALEXIS Was it you, infamous adventurer, who co-operated in the death of our cousin Veuceslas?

BORDURE Sire, grant me your pardon, I was drawn into it by Père Ubu in spite of myself.

ALEXIS Oh what a shocking liar! Never mind, what do you want?

BORDURE Père Ubu had me imprisoned on the pretext of conspiracy; I managed to escape, and galloped my horse for five days and five nights across the steppes to come and implore your gracious pity

ALEXIS What do you bring me as proof of your submission?

BORDURE My sword — the sword of a soldier of fortune, and a detailed plan of the town of Thorn.

ALEXIS I'll take the sword, but by St. George, burn the plan. I don't wish to owe my victory to a piece of treachery.

BORDURE One of Venceslas' sons, young Bougralas, is still alive. I would do anything to re-establish him.

ALEXIS What was your rank in the Polish Army?

81

BORDURE I was in command of the fifth regiment of Vilna dragoons, and of a company of mercenaries in the service of Père Ubu.

ALEXIS Very well, I'll make you a sub-lieutenant in the 10th Cossack regiment, and woe betide you if you betray me. If you fight well, you shall be rewarded.

BORDURE I don't lack courage, Sire.

ALEXIS Good. Disappear from my presence.

(HE GOES OUT)

UBU'S COUNCIL CHAMBER

PÈRE UBU, MÈRE UBU, PHYNANCIAL ADVISERS.

PÈRE UBU Gentlemen, the session is open, and try and listen properly and keep calm. First of all we shall deal with finance, and then we'll talk about a little system I've invented to bring good weather and exorcise rain.

AN ADVISER That's fine, monsieur Ubu.

MÈRE UBU What an idiotic man.

PÈRE UBU Madame of my shittr, look out, for I shan't tolerate your offensive remarks. I must tell you then, gentlemen, that our finances are not too bad.

A considerable number of dogs in woollen stockings prowls about the streets every morning, and the Salopins are doing wonders. On all sides one sees nothing but burnt-out houses and people bending under the weight of our phynances.

THE ADVISER   And the new taxes, Monsieur Ubu, are they going well?

MÈRE UBU   Not in the least. The tax on marriages has only produced eleven sous so far, even though Père Ubu pursues people everywhere to force them to marry.

PÈRE UBU   By my financial sabre, horn of my gibolets, Madame the financieress, I have earews to speak with and you have a mouth to hear me with. (BURSTS OF LAUGHTER) Or rather, no!

You put me off, and it's your fault that I'm stupid. But Ubu's horns! (A MESSENGER ENTERS) Well, come on, what's the matter with the chap? Get out, oaf, or I'll pocket you with decapitation and wringing of the legs.

MÈRE UBU Ah! he's gone, but there's a letter.

PÈRE UBU Read it. I think I'm going out of my mind, or else I can't

85

read. Hurry up, buffooness, it should be from Bordure.

MÈRE UBU   *Exactly. He says that the Czar has welcomed him very kindly, that he's going to invade your States and re-establish Bougrelas, and that as for you, you'll be killed.*

PÈRE UBU   *Oho! I'm afraid, I'm afraid! Oh! I think I'm going to die. Oh, poor man that I am! What will become of me, great God? That nasty man will kill me. S! Anthony and all the saints, protect me, I'll give you some phynance and burn candles for you. Lord, what will become of me?*

(HE WEEPS AND SOBS)

86

MÈRE UBU There's only one way out, Père Ubu.

PÈRE UBU What's that, my love?

MÈRE UBU War!!

ALL Great God, how noble!

PÈRE UBU Yes, and I'll get knocked about some more.

FIRST COUNSELLOR Hurry, let's hurry and organise the army.

SECOND And collect the provisions.

THIRD And prepare the artillery and fortresses.

FOURTH And get the money for the troops.

87

PÈRE UBU Oh no you don't, not money! I'll kill you. I don't want to give out any money. What next! I used to be paid to make war, and now I've got to make it at my own expense. No, by my green candle, let's go to war, since you are so keen on it, but don't let's pay out a sou.

ALL Hurrah for war!

SCENE 8.

THE CAMP BELOW WARSAW

PALOTINS Long live Poland! Long live Père Ubu!

PÈRE UBU Ah! Mère Ubu, give me my breastplate and my little bit of wood. I shall soon be so

88

weighed down that I shouldn't be able to walk even if I was being chased.

MÈRE UBU Pooh, what a coward!

PÈRE UBU Ah, here's the sabre of shittr running away, and the financial hook that won't stay put. I'll never be ready, and the Russians are advancing and they'll kill me.

A SOLDIER My lord Ubu, the earens-pick has fallen down.

PÈRE UBU   Methinks I killed you with the shitter hook and the cut throat.

PÈRE UBU   Isn't he handsome with his helmet and breastplate, he looks like an armed pumpkin.

PÈRE UBU   Ah! now I'm going to mount my horse. Gentlemen, bring the phynancial horse.

MÈRE UBU   Père Ubu, your horse won't be able to bear your weight, it hasn't had anything to eat for five days and it's half dead.

PÈRE UBU   That's a good one! I have to pay twelve sous a day for this old crock and it can't even bear my weight. What d'you

take me for, Ubu's horns! or
are you robbing me?

(MÈRE UBU BLUSHES AND DROPS HER EYES.)

Then somebody bring me another
beast, but I won't go on foot,
horngibolets.

(AN ENORMOUS HORSE IS BROUGHT)

I'll climb on to it. Oh no, better
sit down, or I'll fall off. (THE HORSE
MOVES OFF) Oh, stop my horse, great
God, I'll fall off and be dedd!!!

MÈRE UBU   He really is an imbecile. Ah, now
he's up again. But he fell off.

PÈRE UBU   Horn of Physics, I'm half dead.
Never mind, I'm going to war
and I'll kill everybody. And
anybody who doesn't obey me-
watch out! I'll put him
in my pocket with wringing of

the neck and teeth and
extraction of the tongue.

MÈRE UBU Good luck, Monsieur Ubu.

PÈRE UBU I forgot to say that I
leave the regency in your
hands. But I've got the
cash book on me, so you'll
regret it if you rob me.
I'll leave you the Palotin
Giron to help you. Adieu, Mère Ubu.

MÈRE UBU Adieu, Père Ubu. Be sure and
kill the Czar.

PÈRE UBU You bet. Wringing of the nose
and teeth, extraction of the
tongue, and driving of the little
bit of wood into the earens.

(THE ARMY MOVES OFF TO THE SOUND OF FANFARES)

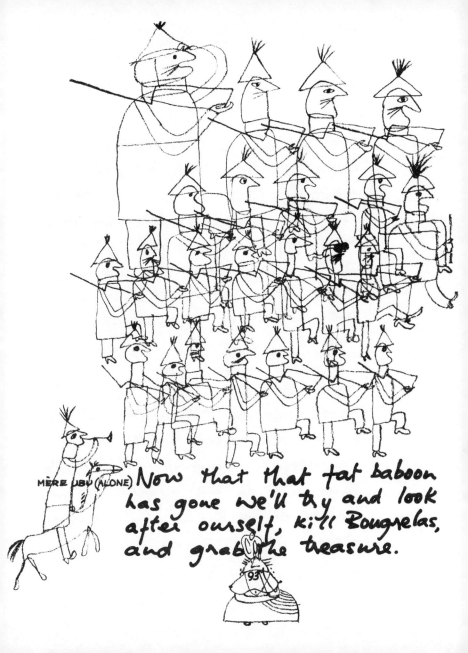

MÈRE UBU (ALONE) Now that that fat baboon has gone we'll try and look after ourself, kill Bougrelas, and grab the treasure.

ACT IV

SCENE 1.

THE CRYPT OF THE FORMER KINGS OF POLAND

IN WARSAW CATHEDRAL

MÈRE UBU   Where on earth is that treasure?
None of the paving stones sounds
hollow. But I know I counted
thirteen stones after the tomb
of Ladislas the Great, keeping
to the wall, but there's nothing
here. Someone must have misled
me. Just a minute, though:
the stone sounds hollow here.
To work, Mère Ubu. Courage,
let's loosen this stone. Let's
get hold of this end of the
financial hook, it'll come
in useful. There it is! There's
the gold in the middle of the
bones of the Kings. Into our
bag with it, then, the whole

lot. Hey! What's that noise?
Could there still be someone
alive in these old vaults? No,
it's nothing, let's hurry up.
We'll take the lot. This money
will be better off in the light
of day than in the middle of
the tombs of ancient princes.
Let's put the stone back.
What's that? Still that noise.
My presence in these haunts
occasions a strange dread in
me. I'll take the rest of this
gold another time; I'll come
back tomorrow.

A VOICE (COMING FROM THE TOMB OF JEAN SIGISMOND)

Never, mère Ubu!

(MÈRE UBU RUNS AWAY TERRIFIED, TAKING THE STOLEN
GOLD AWAY BY THE SECRET DOOR)

THE MAIN SQUARE IN WARSAW

BOUGRELAS AND HIS PARTISANS , PEOPLE AND SOLDIERS.

BOUGRELAS Advance, my friends! Long live Venceslas and Poland. That old rogue of a Père Ubu has gone, only that hag mère Ubu and her Palotin are left. I will march at your head to re-establish the race of my fathers.

ALL Long live Bougrelas.

BOUGRELAS And we will abolish all the taxes imposed by the frightful Père Ub.

ALL Hurrah! Come on! Let's go off to the Palace and do away with all that lot!

BOUGRELAS Hey! Mère Ubu's coming out on to the steps with her guards!

MÈRE UBU What do you want, gentlemen? Oh! It's Bougrelas.

(THE CROWD THROWS STONES)

97

FIRST GUARD   All the windows are broken.

SECOND   St George, I'm done for.

THIRD   Hornsblood, I'm dying.

BOUGRELAS   Throw some stones, my friends.

PALOTIN GIRON   Huh! So that's how it is!

(HE DRAWS HIS SWORD AND RUSHES AT THEM, PRODUCING

A TERRIFYING CARNAGE)

BOUGRELAS   The two of us! Defend yourself, cowardly rascal.

(THEY FIGHT)

GIRON   I die!

98

BOUGRELAS Victory, my friends! Now for mère Ubu

(TRUMPETS ARE HEARD)

Aha! The Nobles are arriving.
Come on, let's get hold of that
horrible hellhag!

ALL Just to go on with, until we
can strangle the old bandit.

(MÈRE UBU RUNS AWAY PURSUED BY ALL THE POLES. RIFLE SHOTS AND A HAIL OF STONES

SCENE 3.

THE POLISH ARMY MARCHING IN THE UKRAINE

PÈRE UBU Hornsblood, godslegs, head of
a bitch! We shall perish,
because we're dying of thirst
and we're tired. Sir Soldier,
be so good as to carry our
financial helmet, and you,
Sir Lancer, take charge of the

99

shith-pick and the constitution
stick to assuage our person
for, I repeat, we are tired.

(THE SOLDIERS OBEY)

PILE

Hey, Monsieuye! It's odd that
the Russians don't put in an
appearance.

PÈRE UBU

It is regrettable that our finances
don't permit of our having a
carriage suitable to our size
for, from fear of demolishing
our mount we have covered
all this distance on foot,
leading our horse by the reins.
But when we are back in
Poland, we shall devise, by means
of our knowledge of the constitution
and aided by the learning of
our counsellors, a wind-carriage
which will be capable of

transporting the whole army.

COTICE Here comes Nicholas Rensky—he seems to be in a hurry.

PÈRE UBU And what's the matter with the fellow?

RENSKY All is lost, Sire. The Poles have revolted, Giron has been killed, and Mère Ubu has taken to flight in the mountains.

PÈRE UBU Nightbird, animal of misfortune, owl in gaiters! Where have you dug up that nonsense? Whatever next! And who's responsible for that? Bougrelas, no doubt. Where have you come from?

RENSKY From Warsaw, noble Lord.

PÈRE UBU Son of my shittr, if *I* believed you *I'd* make the whole army turn back. But, sir son, your nut consists of more feathers than brain, and you've been dreaming a lot of tripe. Off you go to the outposts, my son, the Russians aren't far off, and we shall soon have to be letting fly with our arms, with the shittry arms as well as with the phynancial arms and the physical arms.

GEN. LASCY Père Ubu, can't you see the Russians on the plain?

PÈRE UBU *It's* true, the Russians! I'm in a fine mess. If there was still some way out, but not at all, we are on the top of a hill and we'll be exposed to every blow.

THE ARMY The Russians! The enemy!

PÈRE UBU Come, gentlemen, we must
make our preparations for the
battle. We'll stay on the hill
and we won't be so daft as
to go down to the bottom.
I'll stay in the middle, like
a living stronghold, and you
others revolve around me.
I must advise you to put as
many bullets in your guns as
they will hold, for eight bullets
can kill eight Russians, and
I'll have that amount less to
deal with. We'll have the infantry
on foot at the bottom of the hill
to receive the Russians and
kill them a bit, the cavalry

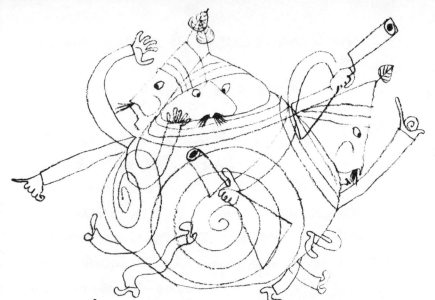

behind to throw themselves
into the confusion, and the
artillery around that windmill
over there to fire into the lot.
As for us, we'll take our place
inside the windmill, and we'll
shoot through the window
with the phynancial pistol,
we'll put the constitution stick
across the door, and if anyone

tries to come in he'd better look out for the shittr hook!

OFFICERS Your orders, Sire Ubu, shall be executed.

PÈRE UBU Ha! that's right, we shall be victorious. What's the time?

GEN. LASCY Eleven a.m.

PÈRE UBU Well then, we'll go and have dinner, for the Russians won't attack before midday. Tell the soldiers, my Lord General, to relieve themselves and to strike up the Financial song.

(LASCY GOES OUT)

SOLDIERS Long live Père Ubu, our great Financier! Tang, tang, tang; tang tang, tang; tang, tang, tang, tatang!

PÈRE UBU   Oh the gallant fellows, I adore them!

(A RUSSIAN CANNON BALL ARRIVES AND BREAKS THE SAIL

OF THE WINDMILL)

Oh! I'm afraid, Lord God, i'm dead!
but no, all the same, I'm all right.

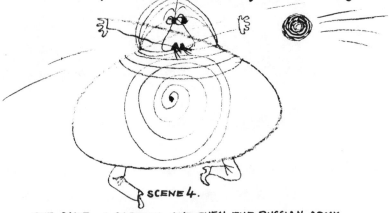

SCENE 4.

THE SAME, A CAPTAIN, AND THEN THE RUSSIAN ARMY.

A CAPTAIN (ARRIVING) Sire Ubu, the Russians are
attacking.

PÈRE UBU   Well, what of it, what do you
want me to do about it? I
didn't tell them to attack.
Nevertheless, Financial Gentlemen,

we will prepare ourselves for battle.

GEN. LASCY   A second cannon ball!

PÈRE UBU   Oh! I can't stand it any longer. It's raining lead and iron in these parts and we might damage our precious person. Let's go down.

(ALL DESCEND AT THE DOUBLE. THE BATTLE HAS JUST BEGUN. THEY DISAPPEAR IN COLUMNS OF SMOKE AT THE FOOT OF THE HILL.)

A RUSSIAN (STRIKING)
For God and the Czar!

RENSKY   Ah! I am dead.

PÈRE UBU   Forward! Hey you, Monsieur let me get hold of you, you've hurt me, do you hear? toper!

107

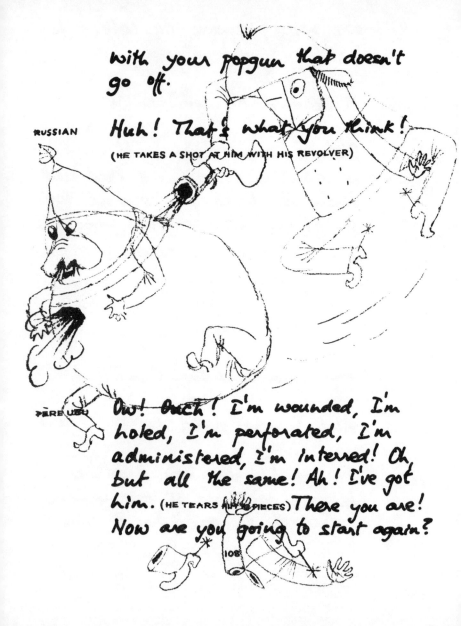

with your popgun that doesn't go off.

RUSSIAN Huh! That's what you think!

(HE TAKES A SHOT AT HIM WITH HIS REVOLVER)

PÈRE UBU Ow! Ouch! I'm wounded, I'm holed, I'm perforated, I'm administered, I'm interred! Oh, but all the same! Ah! I've got him. (HE TEARS HIM TO PIECES) There you are! Now are you going to start again?

GEN. LASCY
Forward, push on with vigour, cross the ditch. Victory is ours.

PÈRE UBU
Think so? So far i've felt more bruises than laurels on my brow.

RUSSIAN CAVALRY
Hurrah! make way for the Czar.

(THE CZAR ARRIVES, ACCOMPANIED BY BORDURE IN DISGUISE)

A POLE
Oh Lord! Every man for himself, here's the Czar!

ANOTHER
Oh good God, he's crossed the ditch.

ANOTHER
Bang bang! that's four done for by that great clodhopper of a lieutenant.

BORDURE
What! haven't you given up yet, you lot? Here, Jean Sobiesky, here's your reckoning! (HE KILLS HIM)

109

Now for the others!

(HE SLAUGHTERS MORE POLES)

PÈRE UBU Come on, my friends! Grab hold of this lout - make mincemeat of the Muscovites! Victory is ours! Long live the Red Eagle.

ALL Come on! Hurrah! Godslegs! Grab hold of the big oaf.

BORDURE By St George, I'm fallen.

PÈRE UBU (RECOGNISING HIM) Aha! it's you, Bordure! Ha! my friend. We, and all the company, are very happy to meet you again. I'm going to cook you by inches. Light the fire, Financial Gentlemen. Oh! Ah! Oh! I'm dead.

It must be at least a cannon ball that's hit me. Ah! my God, forgive me my sins. Yes, it's certainly a cannon ball.

BORDURE It's a blank cartridge from a pistol.

PÈRE UBU Huh! You'd make fun of me, would you! Again! Into my pocket with him.

(HE FLINGS HIMSELF ON HIM AND TEARS HIM TO PIECES)

GEN. LASCY Père Ubu, we're advancing on all fronts.

PÈRE UBU I can see that. I can't go on any longer. I'm riddled with kicks. I think I'll sit down on the ground. Oh, my bottle!

GEN. LASCY Go and take the Czar's, Père Ubu.

PÈRE UBU Hm? I will, this minute. Come on, sabre of shitts, do your duty, and you, financial hook, don't be backward. Let the constitution stick work with noble rivalry, and share with the little bit of wood the honour of slaying, hollowing out and exploiting the Muscovite Emperor! Forward, Monsieur our financial horse! (HE FLINGS HIMSELF ON THE CZAR)

A RUSSIAN OFFICER On guard, Majesty!

PÈRE UBU Here, you! Oh! Ow! Ah! But all the same! Oh, Monsieur, excuse me, leave me alone. Oh! but I didn't do it on purpose!

(HE RUNS AWAY. THE CZAR PURSUES HIM.)

112

Holy Virgin! This madman is chasing me! What have I done, great God! Oh my goodness! There's still the ditch to cross. Oh! I can feel him behind me and the ditch in front. Courage, let's shut our eyes!

(HE JUMPS THE DITCH. THE CZAR FALLS IN.)

THE CZAR Oh my goodness, I'm in it!

THE POLES Hurrah! The Czar has fallen.

PÈRE UBU Oo, I scarcely dare turn round. He's in it. Oh, that's good, and they're on him. Come on then, Poles, go to it with all your might, he can take it, the wretch! As for me, I don't dare to look at him. But all

113

the same our prediction has
completely come true, the
constitution stick has done
wonders, and there's no doubt
about it, I should have completely
killed him if an inexplicable
terror had not come to
struggle with and annul in
us the effects of our courage.
But we suddenly had to
turn tail, and we owe our
salvation to our adroitness
as a horseman, as well as to
the solidity of the hocks of
our financial horse, whose
rapidity is only equalled by
it's solidity and whose light-
footedness is its celebrity, as
well as to the depth of the
ditch which happened, highly
opportunely, to be situated

114

under the feet of the enemy
of us here present, Master of
Phynances. All this is very
fine, but no one's listening.
But come on now, they're at
it again.

(THE RUSSIAN DRAGOONS CHARGE AND RESCUE THE CZAR)

GEN. LASCY   This time it's a* rout.

PÈRE UBU   Hm! this is the moment to
do a bunk. Now then, Messieurs
the Poles, advance! or rather, retreat!

POLES   Every man for himself!

PÈRE UBU   Come on, on your way. What
a gang, what a retreat, what
a crowd, how'm I going to get
out of this mess? (HE IS JOSTLED)
Hey, you! be careful, or you'll
experience the fiery valour

115

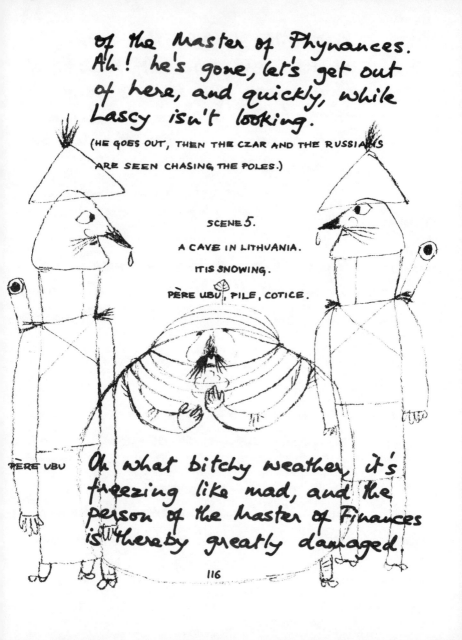

PILE Hey, Monsieuye Ubu, have you got over your terror and your flight?

PÈRE UBU Yes, I'm not frightened any more, but I'm still fleeing.

COTICE (ASIDE) What a swine!

PÈRE UBU Hey, Sire Cotice, your earen, how is it?

COTICE As well, Monsieur, as it can be when it's not well at all. As a conseyquence of the whiche, the lead pushes it over towards the ground, and I haven't been able to extract the bullet.

PÈRE UBU Well that's all right. You were always wanting to beat

117

up other people. As for me,
I've displayed the greatest
valour, and without exposing
myself I've slain four enemies
with my own hands, without
counting all those who were
already dead and whom we
finished off.

COTICE   Do you know, Pile, what
happened to little Rensky?

PILE   He got a bullet through his
head.

PÈRE UBU   As the poppy and the dandelion
in the flower of their age are
scythed by the pitiless scythe
of the pitiless scyther who
pitilessly scythes their pitiful
mugs, so little Rensky has

played the role of the poppy -
he fought mighty well, though,
but there were also too
many Russians.

PILE AND COTICE   Hey, Monsieur!

ECHO   Gurrhey!

PILE   What is it? Let's protect
ourselves with our stecletttos.

PÈRE UBU   Oh! no! blimey! more Russians
I bet! I've had enough! but
it's quite simple, if they get me
I'll putten them in my pocket.

SCENE 6.

THE SAME. ENTER A BEAR.

COTICE   Hey, Monsieur of Finances!

119

PÈRE UBU Oh I say, look at the little bow-wow. Isn't he sweet.

PILE Look out! Phew, what an enormous bear. My cartridges!

PÈRE UBU A bear! Pooh, what a dreadful beast. Oh, poor man, I'm eaten up. God protect me. And he's going for me. No, it's Cotice he's got hold of. Whew! I can breathe again.

(THE BEAR THROWS ITSELF ON COTICE. PILE ATTACKS IT WITH A KNIFE, UBU TAKES REFUGE ON A ROCK.)

COTICE Save me, Pile, save me! help, Monsieur Ubu!

PÈRE UBU Nothing doing! Look after yourself, my friend; just at

The moment we're saying our Pater Noster. Everyone his turn to be eaten.

PILE I've got him, I've got hold of him.

COTICE Hold tight, friend, he's beginning to let go of me.

PÈRE UBU Sanctificetur nomen tuum.

COTICE Bloody coward!

PILE Oh! it's biting me. Oh, Lord save us, I'm dead.

PÈRE UBU Fiat voluntas tua!

COTICE Ah! I've managed to wound it.

PILE Hurrah! it's bleeding.

(IN THE MIDDLE OF THE CRIES OF THE PALOTINS, THE BEAR ROARS AND UBU CONTINUES TO MUMBLE.)

COTICE Hang on while *I* get hold of my explosive knuckk-duster.

PÈRE UBU Panem nostrum quotidianum da nobis hodie.

PILE Haven't you got it yet? I can't hold out.

PÈRE UBU Sicut et nos dimittimus debitoribus nostris.

COTICE Ah! I've got it.

(THERE IS THE SOUND OF AN EXPLOSION AND THE BEAR FALLS DEAD.)

PILE & COTICE Victory!

122

PÈRE UBU Sed libera nos a malo. Amen. Well, is it good and dead? Can I come down from my rock?

PILE (CONTEMPTUOUSLY) When you like.

PÈRE UBU (COMING DOWN) You can pride yourselves that if you are still living, and if you still trample underfoot the snow of Lithuania, you owe it to the noble-minded virtue of the Master of Finances, who strained himself to the uttermost, broke his back, and bawled himself hoarse to churn out paternosters for your salvation, and who wielded the spiritual weapon of prayer with a courage equal to the skill you showed in wielding the temporal weapon of the here-present Palotin Cotice, the explosive knuckle-duster. We even carried our devotion further, for we did not hesitate to climb on to a higher rock so that our prayers would have less distance to travel to reach the heavens.

PILE

Revolting oaf!

PÈRE UBU

What a great blockhead you are. Thanks to me you have something to sup off. What a stomach, gentlemen! The Greeks would have been more comfortable in there than in the wooden horse and, dear friends, we were very nearly able to verify with our own eyes the capacity of its inside.

PILE   I'm dying of hunger. What can we eat?

COTICE   The bear!

PÈRE UBU   Hey, you poor things, are you going to eat it raw? We've nothing to make a fire with.

PILE   We have our gun-flints, haven't we?

PÈRE UBU   Hm, that's true. What's more, it seems to me that there's a little wood not far from here where there should be some dry branches. Go and fetch

125

some, Sire Cotice.

(COTICE GOES OFF ACROSS THE SNOW)

PILE

And now, Sire Ubu, you go and cut up the bear.

PÈRE UBU

Oh no. It may not be dead. Whereas you've already been half eaten and bitten all over, it's entirely your business. I'll go and light the fire while he's bringing the wood.

(PILE BEGINS TO CUT UP THE BEAR)

PÈRE UBU

Oh! look out! it moved!

PILE

But Sire Ubu, it's already cold.

PÈRE UBU

That's a pity, it would have been better to eat it warm. This is going to give the Master of Finances indigestion.

126

PILE (ASIDE) It's revolting. (ALOUD) Help us a bit, Monsieur Ubu, I can't do everything.

PÈRE UBU No, I don't want to do anything. I'm tired, my goodness.

COTICE (COMING BACK) What snow, my fiends, anyone would think we were in Castile or at the North Pole. The light's going. In an hour it will be completely dark. Let's hurry up while we can still see.

PÈRE UBU Yes, do you hear, Pile? hurry up. Hurry up both of you! Put the beast on the spit, cook the beast, I'm hungry.

PILE Oh! that's really too much!

127

you'll have to work on you won't have any, d'you hear, greedy-guts?

PÈRE UBU   Oh! I don't mind. I'd just as soon eat it raw, then you'll be had. Anyway, I'm sleepy.

COTICE   What can we do, Pile? Let's make the dinner by ourselves. He won't have any, that's all. Or we could give him the bones.

PILE   Right. Ah, the fire's burning up.

PÈRE UBU   Oh, that's good, now it's warm. But I can see the Russians everywhere. What a retreat, great God! Ah! (HE FALLS ASLEEP)

COTICE   I'd like to know if what Rensky

128

said is true, if mère Ubu is really dethroned. It wouldn't be impossible.

PILE Let's finish making the supper.

COTICE No, we have things to talk about which are more important. I think it would be a good idea to enquire into the truth of this.

PILE It's true; should we abandon Père Ubu or stay with him?

COTICE Let's sleep on it, then we'll know what to do tomorrow.

PILE No, it would be better to take advantage of the night to make our escape.

COTICE Let's go then. (THEY GO)

SCENE 7.

UBU (TALKING IN HIS SLEEP)

Ah, Sire Russian dragoon, look out, don't fire in this direction, there's someone here. Ah! there's Bordure, how unpleasant he is, you'd think he was a bear. And here's Bougrelas coming after me! The bear, the bear! Ah, it's down! How tough it is, great God! ? don't want to do anything. Go away, Bougrelas! Do you hear, scoundrel? Here's Rensky now, and the Czar! Oh, they're going to fight me. And Ma Ubu! Where did you get all that gold? You've pinched my gold, you trollop, you've been ferreting around

130

in my tomb in Warsaw Cathedral,
near the moon. I've been dead
a long time, Bougrelas killed me,
and I'm buried in Warsaw
near Vladislas the Great, and
also in Cracow, near Jean
Sigismond, and also in Thorn,
in the dungeon with Bordure.
There it is again. But will
you go away, accursed bear!
You look like Bordure. Do
you hear, satanic beast? No,
he doesn't hear, the Salopins
have cut off his earens.
Disembrain them, killen them,
cut their earens off, seize their
cash and drink yourself to
death, that's the life for a
Salopin, and that's happiness
for the Master of Finances.

(HE FALLS SILENT AND SLEEPS)

131

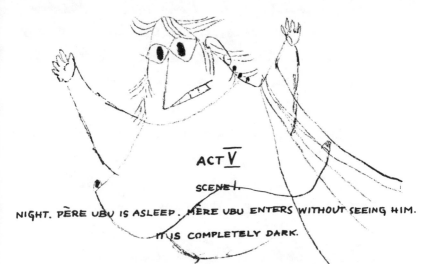

ACT <u>V</u>

SCENE I.

NIGHT. PÈRE UBU IS ASLEEP. MÈRE UBU ENTERS WITHOUT SEEING HIM.

IT IS COMPLETELY DARK.

MÈRE UBU   At last I've reached shelter. I'm alone here, that's not a bad thing, but what a frightful journey: imagine crossing the whole of Poland in four days! Every misfortune assailed me at the same time. The moment that great oaf has gone, I go off to the crypt to make my fortune. Soon afterwards I'm nearly stoned

to death by that Bougrelas
and his madmen. I lose my
escort, the Palotin Giron, who was
so enamoured of my attractions
that he went into raptures
whenever he saw me and even,
I was assured, whenever he
didn't see me, which is the greatest
proof of love. He'd have had
himself cut in two for me, poor
boy. The proof is that he was
cut in four by Bougrelas.
Bang, bang, bang! Oh, I thought
I should die. After that, then,
I take to my heels, pursued by
the enraged crowd. I leave
the Palace, I arrive at the Vistula,
all the bridges were guarded.
I swim across the river, hoping
thus to tire my persecutors.
From all sides the nobility

rallies and pursues me. I nearly perish a thousand times, smothered in a circle of Poles bent on destroying me. At last I cheated their fury, and after a four days' journey in the snow of what was my kingdom, I arrive here to take refuge. I've neither drunk nor eaten these four days. Bougrelas was close on my heels... Still, here I am, saved. Ah! I'm dead with fatigue and cold. But I'd really like to know what happened to my fat buffoon — I mean to say my very respectable spouse. Have I taken his cash! Have I pinched his rix-dollars! Have I diddled him! And his financial horse that was dying of hunger; he didn't see many oats, the poor devil. Oh, what a joke! But alas! I've lost my treasure! It's in Warsaw, anyone who likes can go and fetch it.

PÈRE UBU (BEGINNING TO WAKE UP) Catch Mère Ubu, cut off her earens!

MÈRE UBU Oh God! Where am I? I'm going off my head. Oh no, Lord!

By the grace of God
I can just see
Monsieur Père Ubu
who sleeps quite near to me.

Let's pretend to be nice. Well, my old fellow, did you sleep well?

135

PÈRE UBU Darned badly! It was very tough, that bear! Conflict between voracious creatures and coriaceous creatures, but the voracious completely ate up and devoured the coriaceous, as you will see when it gets light. Do you hear, noble Palotins?

MÈRE UBU What's he burbling about? He's even more of a fool than when he went away. Who's he grumbling at?

PÈRE UBU Cotice, Pile, answer me, sack of shitt! Where are you? Oh, I'm frightened! But after all, someone spoke. Who spoke? Not the bear, I suppose. Shitt! Where are my matches? Oh! I lost them in the battle.

MÈRE UBU (ASIDE) Let's take advantage of the situation and of the night; let's pretend to be a supernatural apparition, and make him promise to pardon our bit of pilfering.

PÈRE UBU But by S! Anthony, someone's speaking. Godslegs! May I be hanged!

MÈRE UBU (AMPLIFYING HER VOICE) Yes, Monsieur Ubu, someone is indeed speaking, and the archangel's trumpet that will call the dead from their final dust and ashes will not speak otherwise! Listen to this stern voice. It's the voice of S! Gabriel, who cannot give other than good advice.

PÈRE UBU Oh *I* say!

MÈRE UBU Don't interrupt me, or *I* shall cease speaking, and it'll be all up with your gutskins!

PÈRE UBU Oh my gibolets! *I'll* be quiet, *I* won't breathe a word. Continue, Madame Apparition.

MÈRE UBU We were saying, Monsieur Ubu, that you were a fat fellow.

PÈRE UBU Very fat indeed, that's fair enough.

MÈRE UBU Hold your tongue, by God!

PÈRE UBU Oh! Angels don't swear!

MÈRE UBU (ASIDE) Shitrr! (CONTINUING) Are you married, Monsieur Ubu?

138

PÈRE UBU Certainly, to the vilest of old hags!

MÈRE UBU You mean that she is a charming woman.

PÈRE UBU A horror. She has claws all over her, you don't know how to get at her.

MÈRE UBU You must approach her gently, Sire Ubu, and if you approach her thus you will see that she is at least the equal of Diana of the Ephesians.

PÈRE UBU Who did you say's got fleas on 'em?

MÈRE UBU You are not listening, Monsieur Ubu, lend us a more attentive ear. (ASIDE) But we must hurry,

139

the dawn is breaking. Monsieur Ubu, your wife is adorable and delicious, she has not a single defect.

PÈRE UBU You're mistaken, there's not a defect that she doesn't possess.

MÈRE UBU Be silent, will you? Your wife isn't unfaithful to you.

PÈRE UBU I'd like to see who could be in love with her. She's an old hell-cat!

MÈRE UBU She doesn't drink!

PÈRE UBU Not since I took the key of the cellar. Before, at eight in the morning she was boozed and perfumed with brandy.

Now that she perfumes herself with heliotrope she doesn't smell any worse. It's all the same to me. But now it's only I who get boozed!

MÈRE UBU Foolish creature! Your wife doesn't take your gold.

PÈRE UBU No, that's odd!

MÈRE UBU She doesn't pinch a sou!

PÈRE UBU As witness our noble and unfortunate Phynancial horse who, not having been nourished for three months, had to go through the entire campaign led by the reins across the Ukraine. And thus he died in harness, the poor creature!

141

MÈRE UBU All that is a pack of lies, your wife is a model, and you, what a monster you are!

PÈRE UBU All that is the truth. My wife is a slut, and you, what a dope you are!

MÈRE UBU Be careful, Père Ubu!

PÈRE UBU Oh, that's true, I forgot who I was talking to. No, I didn't say that.

MÈRE UBU You killed Venceslas.

PÈRE UBU Yes, but it wasn't my fault. It was Mère Ubu who wanted me to.

MÈRE UBU You were responsible for the

142

deaths of Boleslas and Ladislas.

PÈRE UBU — Too bad for them! They were trying to touch me.

MÈRE UBU — You didn't keep your promise to Bordure, and then you killed him.

PÈRE UBU — I'd rather it was I than he to reign in Lithuania. At the moment it's neither the one nor the other. So you see, it's not I.

MÈRE UBU — There is only one way for you to be pardoned your misdeeds.

PÈRE UBU — What's that? I'm quite prepared to become a holy man, I'd

143

like to be a bishop and see
my name in the calendar
of saints.

MÈRE UBU You must forgive Mère Ubu for
having side-tracked a little money.

PÈRE UBU Well, this is what I'll do; I'll
forgive her when she's given
it all back, when she's had
a good beating, and when
she's brought my financial
horse back to life.

MÈRE UBU He's crazy about that horse
of his! Oh, I'm lost, it's getting
light.

PÈRE UBU But still, I'm glad to know
for certain that my dear
spouse robbed me. Now

I have it on the highest authority. Omnis a Deo scientia, which means: omnis, all; a Deo, knowledge; scientia, comes from God. That's the explanation of the phenomenon. But Madame Apparition doesn't say any more. What can I offer her to cheer her up? What she told me was very amusing. Ah, but the day has dawned! Oh Lord, by my financial horse, it's Mère Ubu.

MÈRE UBU (BRAZENING IT OUT) It's not true, I shall excommunicate you.

PÈRE UBU Pah! you slut!

MÈRE UBU What impiety!

PÈRE UBU   Oh, that's a bit much! I can see very well that it's you, you silly bitch! Why the devil are you here?

MÈRE UBU   Giron is dead and the Poles chased me out.

PÈRE UBU   Well, it was the Russians who chased me out: great minds think alike.

MÈRE UBU   This great mind thinks it's met an ass.

PÈRE UBU   Ah well, it's going to think it's met a palmiped in a minute. (HE THROWS THE BEAR AT HER)

MÈRE UBU   (FALLING DOWN OVERWHELMED BY THE WEIGHT OF THE BEAR) Oh, great God, how frightful!

146

Ah, I'm dying! I'm suffocating! it's biting me! It's swallowing me! it's digesting me!

PÈRE UBU It's dead, grotesque hag! Oh, but come to think of it, perhaps it's not! Oh Lord no, it's not dead, let's make ourself scarce. (CLIMBING ON HIS ROCK AGAIN) Pater noster qui es...

MÈRE UBU (EXTRICATING HERSELF) Hm! Where is he?

PÈRE UBU Oh Lord, there she is again! Daft creature, isn't there any way of getting rid of her? Is that bear dead?

MÈRE UBU Of course it is, you silly

147

ass, it's already quite cold.
How did it get here?

PÈRE UBU (CONFUSED) I don't know. Oh yes I
do, though. It wanted to
eat Pile and Cotice and I
killed it with one stroke of
a Pater Noster.

MÈRE UBU Pile, Cotice, Pater Noster!
What's he talking about? He's
barmy, my fiancé.

PÈRE UBU What I say is the truth.
And you are an idiot,
my gutskins.

MÈRE UBU Tell me about your campaign,
Père Ubu.

PÈRE UBU Oh God no! It's too long.

All I know is that in spite
of my incontestable valiance,
they all beat me.

MÈRE UBU   What, even the Poles?

PÈRE UBU   They shouted: Long live Venceslas
and Bougrelas! I thought
they wanted to quarter me.
Oh, the madmen! And then
they killed Rensky.

MÈRE UBU   That's all the same to me!
You know that Bougrelas
killed the Palotin Giron?

PÈRE UBU   That's all the same to me!
And then they killed poor Lascy.

MÈRE UBU   That's all the same to me!

PÈRE UBU Oh, but just a minute, bring yourself here, sloven! Get down on your knees before your master.

(HE GRABS HER AND THROWS HER ON TO HER KNEES)

You're going to undergo the worst torture

MÈRE UBU Ho ho, Monsieur Ubu!

PÈRE UBU Oh! Oh! Oh! What next, have you finished? I'm only just beginning: twisting of the nose, pulling out of the hair, shoving of the little bit of wood in the earens, extraction of the brain by the heels, laceration of the posterior, partial, or even total, suppression of the spinal marrow (if at least that would remove the spines

150

from her character), not forgetting
the opening of the swimming bladder,
and finally the grand new
version of the beheading of
St. John the Baptist, the whole
taken from the very holy scriptures,
from the Old as well as from
the New Testament, arranged,
corrected and perfected by
the here-present Master of
Finances. Does that suit you,
chucklehead?

(HE BEGINS TO TEAR HER TO PIECES)

MÈRE UBU Mercy, Monsieur Ubu!

(LOUD NOISE IN THE ENTRANCE TO THE CAVE)

THE SAME ; BOUGRELAS , RUSHING INTO THE CAVE WITH HIS SOLDIERS.

BOUGRELAS Forward, my friends! Long live Poland!

PÈRE UBU Hey hey! wait a bit, Monsieur the Polognard. Wait till i've finished with Madame my better half.

BOUGRELAS (STRIKING HIM) Take that, coward, vagabond, braggart, miscreant, mussalman!

PÈRE UBU (COUNTERING) Take that, Polognard, drunkard, bastard, hussar, tartar, dozener, cozener, liar, Savoyard, communard!

MÈRE UBU (BEATING HIM AS WELL) Take that!

Swindler, porker, traitor, play-
actor, perjurer, dog-robber,
bolster!

(THE SOLDIERS FLING THEMSELVES ON THE UBS
WHO DEFEND THEMSELVES AS BEST THEY CAN)

PÈRE UBU   ye gods, what a bashing!

MÈRE UBU We have feet, Messieurs the Poles.

PÈRE UBU By my green candle! I say, are they going to have done, when all's said and done. What, another! Ah! if I had my financial horse here!

BOUGRELAS Hit 'em, go on hitting 'em!

VOICES OFF Long live Père Ubu, our great Financier!

PÈRE UBU Ah! here they are! Hurrah! Here come the Père Ubists. Come on, forward march, we can do with you, Financial Gentlemen!

(THE PALOTINS ENTER AND THROW THEMSELVES INTO THE MÊLÉE.)

154

COTICE   Outside, Poles!

PILE   Ah! we meet again, Monsieur of Finances. Come on, press on, we must get out; once outside we'll simply make ourselves scarce.

PÈRE UBU   Oh, ouch! that's the worst yet. Ow, he can't half hit!

BOUGRELAS   God! I am wounded.

STANISLAS LECZINSKI   It's nothing, Sire.

BOUGRELAS   No, I'm only stunned.

JEAN SOBIESKI   Hit them, go on hitting them, they're escaping.

COTICE   We're getting there, follow your

leader. By conseyquence of the whiche I see the Heavens opening out ~~before~~ me.

PILE

Courage, Sire Ubu!

PÈRE UBU

Hell! I'm doing it in my breeches. ~~Get~~ a move on, horngibolets! Killem 'em, bleed 'em, skin 'em, massacre 'em, Ubu's horns! Ah, it's dying down.

COTICE

There are only two left guarding the entrance.

PÈRE UBU (KILLING THEM WITH BLOWS WITH THE BEAR)

And a one, and a two! Oof! I'm outside! Let's clear out! Follow me, you lot, and look sharp!

156

THE STAGE REPRESENTS THE PROVINCE OF LIVONIA COVERED WITH

SNOW. THE UBS AND THEIR SUITE IN FLIGHT.

PÈRE UBU Ah! I think they've given up trying to catch us.

MÈRE UBU Yes, Bougrelas has gone to get himself crowned.

PÈRE UBU I don't envy him his crown.

MÈRE UBU You're dead right, Père Ubu.

(THEY DISAPPEAR INTO THE DISTANCE.)

157

SCENE 4.

THE BRIDGE OF A SHIP

SAILING CLOSE TO THE WIND ON THE BALTIC.

ON THE BRIDGE, PÈRE UBU AND ALL HIS GANG.

CAPTAIN

Oh what a lovely breeze!

PÈRE UBU

It's a fact that we're moving with a rapidity that savours of the marvellous. We must be doing at least a million knots an hour, and these knots have this to recommend them, that once done they don't come undone. It's true that we have a fair wind.

PILE

What a sorry imbecile!

(A SQUALL ARRIVES, THE SHIP HEELS OVER AND THE SPRAY FLIES.)

158

PÈRE UBU Oh! Ah! God! We're capsizing. But it's going all skew, your boat, it's going to fall over.

CAPTAIN Everyone to leeward, set the foresail.

PÈRE UBU Oh hell no! don't all go over to the same side! That's very unwise. And supposing the wind changes: we'll all go down to the bottom of the sea and the fishes will eat us.

CAPTAIN Fall off!

PÈRE UBU What do you mean, fall off! I don't want to fall off, I want to get there, I'm in a hurry. Don't fall off, do you hear?

It's all your fault, brute of a captain, if we don't get there. We ought to be there already. Oh, oh! but I'm going to take command. Ready about! 'bout ship! Let go the anchor, go about in stays, wear ship, hoist the sails, haul down the sails, helm up, helm down, helm sideways, you see, it's going a treat. Bring the ship athwart the waves, and that'll be perfect.

(ALL ARE CONVULSED WITH LAUGHTER; THE BREEZE FRESHENS)

160

CAPTAIN   Haul down the main jib, reef the topsails.

PÈRE UBU   That's not bad, that's even good. Do you hear, Monsieur the Crew? Haul down the main bib and reach for your tonsils.

(SEVERAL DIE OF LAUGHING. A WAVE IS SHIPPED)

Oh - what a deluge. That's the result of the manœuvres we ordered.

PILE AND MÈRE UBU   What a delicious thing navigation is!

(SECOND WAVE SHIPPED)

PILE (DRENCHED)   Beware of Satan and his pumps and vanities!

PÈRE UBU Sire steward, bring us something to drink.

MÈRE UBU Ah, what a delight it will be to see our sweet France again soon, our old friends and our castle of Mondragon!

PÈRE UBU Mm, we'll soon be there. We are just below the castle of Elsinore at the moment.

PILE I feel quite cheered up at the idea of seeing my dear Spain again.

COTICE Yes, and we'll dazzle our compatriots with tales of our marvellous adventures.

PÈRE UBU Hm! I should think so! And I'll get myself nominated

162

Master of Finances in Paris.

MÈRE UBU   That's right! Oh, isn't she
pitching about!

COTICE   It's nothing, we've just passed
the Elsinore foreland.

PILE   And how our noble ship leaps
forward over the sombre waves
of the North Sea.

PÈRE UBU   Fierce and inhospitable sea
that laves the country called
Germania, thus named because
all its inhabitants are
cousins-german.

MÈRE UBU   That's what I call erudition.
They say it's a very beautiful
country.

PÈRE UBU Ah, gentlemen! however beautiful it may be, it can never equal Poland. If there weren't any Poland, there wouldn't be any Poles!

END

164

And now, since you have listened very nicely, and behaved yourselves, we are going to sing you:

THE SONG OF THE DISEMBRAINING

paris
1898

I'd worked as a cabinet maker for more than one decade.
Rue du Champ de Mars, (All Saints), was my address.
My wife worked as well; millinery was her trade,
And everything we had was always of the best.
When Sunday came around and we saw it wasn't raining
We use to doll up like mad and make ourselves look fine,
And then we'd all go out to watch the disembraining
Rue de l'Échaudé, to have a lovely time.

> Look, look at the machine revolving,
> Look, look at the brain flying,
> Look, look at the Rentiers trembling!
> *(Chorus)* Hurrah, arse-horns, long live Père Ubu!

Our two dear little brats, smeared all over with jam,
Trustfully brandishing dolls made out of papier maché,
Installed themselves with us on the top of the tram,
And we merrily lurched along towards the Échaudé.
We rushed headlong en masse as near as we could to the fence—
As long as we got to the front, kicks didn't matter two hoots,
I climbed on a heap of stones—*I've* got plenty of sense;
I didn't want the blood to dirty my beautiful boots.

                    Look, look at the machine revolving,
                    Look, look at the brain flying,
                    Look, look at the Rentiers trembling!
       (*Chorus*) Hurrah, arse-horns, long live Père Ubu!

Soon we were white with brain, my loving wife and I.
The brats were eating it up, and we were as merry as hell
At the sight of the Palotin waving his blade sky-high
And the knives all different sizes, and all the wounds as well.
Suddenly what do I see in the corner near the machine
But the mug of a chap I know; an ugly customer, too—
Old cock, says I to him, you may be looking green,
But you used to pinch my things; I shan't be sorry for you.

                    Look, look at the machine revolving,
                    Look, look at the brain flying,
                    Look, look at the Rentiers trembling!
       (*Chorus*) Hurrah, arse-horns, long live Père Ubu!

All of a sudden I feel my wife give me a shove.
You silly mug, says she; this isn't the time to slack—
Chuck a heap of dung in the fellow's face, my love
—Now's your chance because the Palotin's turned his back.
This really magnificent reasoning leaves me much impressed,
So I summon up all my courage and balance myself on tiptoes,
And I sling a gigantic turd at the Rentier's well-padded chest
—Which eventually flattens itself on the bloody Palotin's nose.

                    Look, look at the machine revolving,
                    Look, look at the brain flying,
                    Look, look at the Rentiers trembling!
       (*Chorus*) Hurrah, arse-horns, long live Père Ubu!

In less than no time at all I find that I've changed my role,
I'm pitchforked over the fence by the furiously angry crowd,
And I'm rushed along arse-over-tip into the big black hole
Whence no one ever comes back—unless they're wrapped up in a shroud
And that's what happens to people who go for their Sunday walk
To the Rue d'Échaudé to watch them disembrain,
And work the pig-pinching machine, or even the tomahawk
—When you set out you're alive, and when you come back you're slain.

> Look, look at the machine revolving,
> Look, look at the brain flying,
> Look, look at the Rentiers trembling!
> (*Chorus*) Hurrah, arse-horns, long live Père Ubu!

QUESTIONS OF THE THEATRE

What conditions are indispensable to the theatre? I don't think we need give any more thought to the question of whether the three unities are necessary or whether the unity of action alone will suffice, and if everything revolves round a single character then the unity of action has had its due. Nor do I think that we can argue either from Aristophanes or Shakespeare if it is the public's susceptibilities that we are supposed to respect. Many editions of Aristophanes have footnotes on every page stating: "The whole of this passage is full of obscene allusions," and one only has to re-read certain of Ophelia's words, and the famous scene (nearly always cut) where a Queen is taking French lessons. Unless we are to model ourselves on Messieurs Augier, Dumas fils, Labiche, etc., whom we have had the misfortune to read, and with profound tedium. It is more likely that the members of the younger generation, though they may have read these gentlemen, have not the slightest recollection of having done so. I do not think there is the slightest reason to give a work dramatic form unless one has invented a character whom one finds it more convenient to let loose on a stage than to analyse in a book.

And anyway, why should the public, which is illiterate by definition, attempt quotations and comparisons? It criticised *Ubu Roi* for being a vulgar imitation of Shakespeare and Rabelais, because "its sets are economically replaced by a placard" and a certain word is repeated. People ought not to be unaware of the fact that it is now more or less certain that never, at least never in Shakespeare's day, have his plays been acted in any other way than with sets and on a relatively perfected stage. Furthermore, people saw *Ubu* as a work written in "old French" because we amused ourselves by printing it in old-style type, and they thought "phynance" was sixteenth-century spelling. I find so much more accurate the remark of one of the Poles in the crowd scenes, who said that in his opinion: "It's just like de Musset, because the set changes so frequently."

It would have been easy to alter *Ubu* to suit the taste of the Paris public by making the following minor changes: the initial word would have been Blast or (Blasttr), the lavatory brush would have been a courtesan's couch, Ubu would have conferred a Knighthood on the Tsar, and several people would have committed adultery—but in that case it would have been filthier.

I intended that when the curtain went up the scene should confront the public like the exaggerating mirror in the stories of Madame Leprince de Beaumont, in which the depraved saw themselves with dragons' bodies, or bulls' horns, or whatever corresponded to their particular vice. It is not surprising that the public should have been aghast at the sight of its ignoble other-self, which it had never before been shown completely. This other self, as Monsieur Catulle Mendès has excellently said, is composed "of eternal human imbecility, eternal lust, eternal gluttony, the vileness of instinct magnified into tyranny; of the sense of decency, the virtues, the patriotism and the ideals peculiar to those who have just eaten their fill." Really, these are hardly the constituents for an amusing play, and the masks demonstrate that the comedy must at the most be the macabre comedy of an English clown, or of a Dance of Death. Before we had Gémier, Lugné-Poe knew the part and wanted to rehearse it *as a tragedy*. And the thing which was the least understood—it was made clear enough, though, and constantly recalled by Mère Ubu's continually repeated: "What an idiotic man! . . . What a sorry imbecile!"—was that Ubu's speeches were not meant to be full of witticisms, as various little Ubists claimed, but of stupid remarks, uttered with all the authority of the Ape. And in any case the public, who protest with bogus scorn that it contains: "Not a scrap of wit from beginning to end," are still less capable of understanding anything profound. We know, from our four years' observation of the public at the Théâtre de l'Oeuvre, that if you're absolutely determined to give the public an inkling of something you must explain it to them beforehand.

The public don't understand *Peer Gynt,* which is one of the simplest plays imaginable; neither do they understand Baudelaire's prose or Mallarmé's precise syntax. They know nothing of Rimbaud, they only heard of Verlaine's existence after he was dead, and they are terrified when they hear *Les Flaireurs* or *Pelléas et Mélisande.* They pretend to think writers

174

and artists a lot of clackpots, and some of them would like to purge all works of art of everything inexplicable and quintessential, of every sign of *superiority,* and to castrate them so that they could have been written by the *public in collaboration.* That is their point of view, and that of certain plagiarists, conscious and unconscious. Have we no right to consider the public from our point of view?—the public who claim that we are madmen suffering from a surfeit of what they regard as hallucinatory sensations produced in us by our exacerbated senses. From our point of view it is they who are the madmen, but of the opposite sort—what the scientists would call idiots. They are suffering from a dearth of sensations, for their senses have remained so rudimentary that they can perceive nothing but immediate impressions. Does progress for them consist in drawing nearer to the brute beast, or in gradually developing their embryonic cerebral convolutions?

Since Art and the public's Understanding are so incompatible, we may well have been mistaken in making a direct attack on the public in *Ubu Roi*; they resented it because they understood only too well, whatever they may say. Ibsen's attack on them went almost unnoticed. It is because the public are a mass—inert, obtuse and passive—that they need to be shaken up from time to time so that we can tell from their bear-like grunts where they are—and also where they stand. They are pretty harmless, in spite of their numbers, because they are fighting against intelligence. Ubu didn't disembrain all the nobles. They are like Cyrano de Bergerac's Icicle-Animal, which does battle with the Fire-Beast—in any case they would melt before they won, but even if they did win they would be only too honoured to hang the corpse of the Sun-Beast up against their mantel-pieces and to allow its rays to illuminate their adipose tissue. It is a being so different from them that its relation to them is like an exterior soul to their bodies.

Light is active and shade is passive, and light is not detached from shade but, given sufficient time, penetrates it. Reviews which used to publish Loti's novels are now printing a dozen pages of Verhaeren and several of Iben's plays.

Time is necessary because people who are older than we—and whom we respect for that reason—have lived among certain works which have the charm of habitual objects for them, and they were born with the souls that match these works, guaranteed to last until eighteen-ninety . . . odd. We shan't try and push them out of our way—we are no longer in the seventeenth century; we shall wait until their souls, which make sense in their own contexts and in that of the hollow mockery of which these people's environment has consisted, have come to a full stop (even though we haven't waited). We too shall become solemn, fat and Ubu-like and shall publish extremely classical books which will probably lead to our becoming mayors of small towns where, when we become academicians, the firemen will present us with Sèvres vases, while they present their moustaches on velvet cushions to our children. And another lot of young people will appear, and consider us completely out of date, and they will write ballads to express their loathing of us, and there is no reasons why this should ever end.

(*This essay was first published in the* Revue Blanche.)

I think the question of whether the theatre should adapt itself to the public, or the public to the theatre, has been settled once and for all. The public only understood, or looked as if they understood, the tragedies and comedies of ancient Greece because they were based on universally known fables which, anyway, were explained over and over again in every play and, as often as not, hinted at by a character in the prologue. Just as nowadays they go to hear the plays of Molière and Racine at the Comédie Française because they are always being played. It is in any case quite certain that their substance escapes them. The theatre has not yet won the liberty of forcibly expelling anyone who doesn't understand, or evacuating the auditorium at each interval before the shouting and smashing begins. But we can content ourselves with the established truth that if people do fight in the theatre it will be a work of popularisation they are fighting over, one that is not in the least original and is therefore more readily accessible than the original. An original work will, at least on the first night, be greeted by a public that remains bemused, and consequently dumb.

Yet the first-night public consists of the people who want to understand!

If we want to lower ourselves to the level of the public there are two things we can do for them—and which *are* done for them. The first is to give them characters who think as they do (a Siamese or Chinese ambassador, seeing *l'Avare,* bet that the miser would be outwitted and his money-box stolen), and whom they understand perfectly. When this is the case they receive two impressions; firstly they think that they must themselves be very witty, as they laugh at what they take to be witty writing— and this never fails to happen to Monsieur Donnay's audiences. Secondly they get the impression that they are participating in the creation of the play, which relieves them of the effort of anticipating what is going to happen. The other thing we can do for them is give them a commonplace sort of plot—write about things that happen all the time to the common man, because the fact is that Shakespeare, Michelangelo or Leonardo da Vinci are somewhat bulky; their diameter is a bit difficult to traverse. Because genius, intelligence, and even talent, are larger than life, and so inaccessible to most people.

If, in the whole universe, there are five-hundred people who, compared with infinite mediocrity, have a touch of Shakespeare and Leonardo in them, is it not only fair to grant these five-hundred healthy minds the same thing that is lavished on Monsieur Donnay's audiences—the relief of not seeing on the stage what they don't understand; the *active* pleasure of participating in the creation of the play, and of anticipation?

What follows is a list of a few things which are particularly horrifying and incomprehensible to the five-hundred, and which clutter up the stage to no purpose; first and foremost, the *décor* and the *actors*.

A décor is a hybrid, neither natural nor artificial. If it were exactly like nature it would be a superfluous duplication . . . (We shall consider the use of nature as décor later.) It isn't artificial, in the sense that it is not, for the five-hundred, the embodiment of the outside world as the play-wright has seen and re-created it.

And in any case it would be dangerous for the poet to impose on a public of artists the décor that he himself would conceive. In any written work there is a hidden meaning, and anyone who knows how to read sees that aspect of it that makes sense for him. But there is hardly anyone for whom a painted backcloth has two meanings, as it is far more arduous to extract the quality from a quality than the quality from a quantity. Every spectator has a right to see a play in a décor which does not clash with his own view of it. For the general public, on the other hand, any "artistic" décor will do, as the masses don't understand anything by themselves, but wait to be told how to see things.

There are two sorts of décor; indoor and outdoor. Both are supposed to represent either rooms or the countryside. We shall not revert to the question, which has been settled once and for all, of the stupidity of *trompe l'oeil.* Let us state that the said *trompe l'oeil* is aimed at people who only see things roughly, that's to say, who don't see at all. It scandalises those who see nature in an intelligent and selective way, as it presents them with a caricature of it by someone who lacks all understanding. Zeuxis deceived the brute beasts, so they say, and Titian deceived an innkeeper.

A décor by someone who can't paint is nearer to an abstract décor, as it gives only essentials. In the same way a simplified décor picks out only relevant aspects.

We tried *heraldic* décors, where a single shade is used to represent a whole scene or act, with the characters "passant" harmonically against the heraldic field. This is a bit puerile, as the said colour can only establish itself against a colourless background (but it is also more accurate, as we have to take into account the general red-green colour-blindness, as well as other idiosyncrasies of perception). A colourless background can be achieved simply, and in a way which is symbolically accurate, by an unpainted backcloth or the reverse side of a set. Each spectator can then conjure up for himself the background he requires, or, better still, if the author knew what he was about, the spectator can imagine that, by a process of exosmosis, what he sees on the stage is the real décor. The placard brought in to mark the changes in place prevents his periodically having recourse to a negative state of mind, because with conventional sets one only becomes aware of them at the moment of their change.

In the conditions we are advocating, each piece of scenery needed for a special purpose—a window to be opened, for instance, or a door to be broken down—becomes a prop and can be brought in like a table or a torch.

The actor adapts his face to that of the character, and he should do the same to his body. The play of his features, his expressions, etc., are caused by various contractions and extensions of the muscles of his face. No one has realised that the muscles remain the same under the make-believe, made-up face, and that Mounet and Hamlet do not have the same zygomatics, even though in anatomical terms we think that they are the same man. Or else people say that the difference is negligible. The actor should use a mask to envelop his head, thus replacing it by the effigy of the CHARACTER. His mask should not follow the masks in the Greek theatre

179

in betokening simply tears or laughter, but should indicate the nature of the character: the Miser, the Waverer, the Covetous Man accumulating crimes . . .

And if the eternal nature of the character is embodied in the mask, we can learn from the kaleidoscope, and particularly the gyroscope, a simple means of *illuminating,* one by one or several at a time, the critical moments.

With the old-style actor, masked only in thinly applied make-up, each facial expression is raised to a power by colour and particularly by relief, and then to cubes and higher powers by LIGHTING.

What we are about to describe was impossible in the Greek theatre as the light was vertical, or at least never sufficiently horizontal, and therefore produced a shadow under every protuberance in the mask; it was a blurred shadow, though, because the light was diffused.

Contrary to the deductions of rudimentary and imperfect logic, there is no clear shadow in those sunny countries, and in Egypt, below the tropic of Cancer, there is hardly a trace of shadow left on the face. The light was reflected vertically as if by the face of the moon, and diffused by both the sand on the ground and the sand suspended in the air.

The *footlights* illumine the actor along the hypotenuse of a right-angled triangle, the actor's body forming one of the sides of the right angle. And as the footlights are a series of luminous points, that's to say a line which, in relation to the narrowness of the front view of the actor, extends indefinitely to right and left of its intersection with the actor's plane, these footlights should be considered as a single point of light situated at an indefinite distance, as if it were *behind* the audience.

It is true that the footlights are less than an infinite distance away, so that one cannot really regard all the rays reflected by the actor (or facial expressions) as travelling along parallel lines. But in practice each spectator sees the character's mask *equally,* with differences which are certainly negligible compared to the idiosyncrasies and different perceptive attitudes of the individual spectator. These differences cannot be attenuated, though they cancel each other out in the audience qua herd, which is what an audience is.

By slow nodding and lateral movements of his head the actor can displace the shadows over the whole surface of his mask. And experience has shown that the six main positions (and the same number in profile, though these are less clear), suffice for every expression. We shall not cite any examples, as they vary according to the nature of the mask, and because everyone who knows how to watch a puppet show will have been able to observe this for himself.

They are simple expressions, and therefore universal. Present-day mime makes the great mistake of using conventional mime language, which is tiring and incomprehensible. An example of this convention is the hand describing a vertical ellipse round the face, and a kiss being implanted on this hand to suggest a beautiful woman—and love. An example of universal gesture is the marionette displaying its bewilderment by starting back violently and hitting its head against a flat.

Behind all these accidentals there remains the essential expression, and the finest thing in many scenes is the impassibility of the mask, which remains the same whether the words it emits are grave or gay. This can only be compared with the solid structure of the skeleton, deep down under its surrounding animal flesh; its histrionic qualities have always been acknowledged.

It goes without saying that the actor must have a special *voice,* the voice that is appropriate to the part, as if the cavity forming the mouth of the mask were incapable of uttering anything other than what the mask would say, if the muscles of its lips could move. And it is better for them not to move, and that the whole play should be spoken in a monotone.

And we have also said that the actor must take on the body appropriate to the part.

Transvestism has been forbidden by the Church and by art. Witness Beaumarchais, who in one of his prefaces wrote: "The young man does not exist who is sufficiently developed to . . ." And since women are beardless and their voices shrill all their lives, a boy of fourteen is traditionally played on the Paris stage by a twenty-year-old woman who, being six years older, has that much more experience. This is small compensation for her ridiculous profile and inaesthetic walk, or for the way the outline of all her muscles it vitiated by adipose tissue, which is odious because it has a function—it produces *milk.*

Given the difference in their brains, a boy of fifteen, if you pick an intelligent one (because the majority of women are vulgar and most boys are stupid, but with a few exceptions), will play his part adequately. The young actor Baron, in Molière's company, is an example, and there is also all the period in the English theatre (and the whole history of the Greek theatre) when no one would have dreamed of trusting a part to a woman.

A few words on natural décors, which exist without duplication if one tries to stage a play in the open air, on the slope of a hill, near a river, which is excellent for the carrying of the voice, especially when there is no awning, even though the sound may be weakened. Hills are all that is necessary, with a few trees for shade. At the moment *Le Diable Marchand de Goutte* is being played out-of-doors, as it was a year ago, and the production was discussed some time ago in the *Mercure* by Alfred Vallette. Three or four years ago Monsieur Lugné-Poe and some friends staged *La Gardienne* at Presles, on the edge of the Isle-Adam forest. In these days of universal cycling it wouldn't be absurd to organise a few very short (from two to five) country performances on summer Sundays of literature which is not too abstract—*King Lear* would be a good example; we do not understand the idea of a people's theatre. The performances should be in places not too far distant, and arrangements should be made for people who come by train, without previous planning. The places in the sun should be free (Monsieur Barrucand was only recently writing about the free theatre), and as for the props, the bare necessities could be transported in one or several automobiles.

(This essay was first published in the Mercure de France, *September 1896.)*

New Directions Paperbooks—A Partial Listing

For complete listing request free catalog from
New Directions, 80 Eighth Avenue, New York 10011
†Bilingual

Aller Retour New York. NDP753.
Big Sur & The Oranges. NDP161.
The Colossus of Maroussi. NDP75.
A Devil in Paradise. NDP765.
Into the Heart of Life. NDP728.
The Smile at the Foot of the Ladder. NDP386.
Y. Mishima, Confessions of a Mask. NDP253.
Death in Midsummer. NDP215.
Frédéric Mistral, The Memoirs. NDP632.
Eugenio Montale, It Depends.† NDP507.
Selected Poems.† NDP193.
Paul Morand, Fancy Goods/Open All Night. NDP567.
Vladimir Nabokov, Nikolai Gogol. NDP78.
Laughter in the Dark. NDP729.
The Real Life of Sebastian Knight. NDP432.
P. Neruda, The Captain's Verses.† NDP345.
Residence on Earth.† NDP340.
Fully Empowered. NDP792.
New Directions in Prose & Poetry (Anthology).
Available from #17 forward to #55.
Robert Nichols, Arrival. NDP437.
J. F. Nims, The Six-Cornered Snowflake. NDP700.
Charles Olson, Selected Writings. NDP231.
Toby Olson, The Life of Jesus. NDP417.
George Oppen, Collected Poems. NDP418.
István Örkeny, The Flower Show/
The Toth Family. NDP536.
Wilfred Owen, Collected Poems. NDP210.
José Emilio Pacheco, Battles in the Desert. NDP637.
Selected Poems.† NDP638.
Michael Palmer, At Passages. NDP803.
Nicanor Parra, Antipoems: New & Selected. NDP603.
Boris Pasternak, Safe Conduct. NDP77.
Kenneth Patchen, Because It Is. NDP83.
Collected Poems. NDP284.
Selected Poems. NDP160.
Ota Pavel, How I Came to Know Fish. NDP713.
Octavio Paz, Collected Poems. NDP719.
A Draft of Shadows.† NDP489.
Selected Poems. NDP574.
Sunstone.† NDP735.
A Tale of Two Gardens. NDP841.
A Tree Within.† NDP661.
Victor Pelevin, The Yellow Arrow. NDP845.
Ezra Pound, ABC of Reading. NDP89.
The Cantos. NDP824.
Confucius. NDP285.
Confucius to Cummings. (Anth.) NDP126.
Diptych Rome-London. NDP783.
Elektra. NDP683.
Guide to Kulchur. NDP257.
Literary Essays. NDP250.
Personae. NDP697.
Selected Cantos. NDP304.
Selected Poems. NDP66.
Caradog Prichard, One Moonlit Night. NDP835.
Eça de Queirós, Illustrious House of Ramires. NDP785.
Raymond Queneau, The Blue Flowers. NDP595.
Exercises in Style. NDP513.
Mary de Rachewiltz, Ezra Pound. NDP405.
Raja Rao, Kanthapura. NDP224.
Herbert Read, The Green Child. NDP208.
P. Reverdy, Selected Poems.† NDP346.
Kenneth Rexroth, An Autobiographical Novel. NDP725.
Classics Revisited. NDP621.
More Classics Revisited. NDP668.
Flower Wreath Hill. NDP724.
100 Poems from the Chinese. NDP192.
100 Poems from the Japanese.† NDP147.
Selected Poems. NDP581.
Women Poets of China. NDP528.
Women Poets of Japan. NDP527.
Rainer Maria Rilke, Poems from
The Book of Hours. NDP408.
Possibility of Being. (Poems). NDP436.
Where Silence Reigns. (Prose). NDP464.
Arthur Rimbaud, Illuminations.† NDP56.
Season in Hell & Drunken Boat.† NDP97.

Edouard Roditi, Delights of Turkey. NDP445.
Jerome Rothenberg, Khurbn. NDP679.
Seedings & Others Poems. NDP828.
Nayantara Sahgal, Rich Like Us. NDP665.
Ihara Saikaku, The Life of an Amorous Woman.
NDP270.
St. John of the Cross, Poems.† NDP341.
William Saroyan, Fresno Stories. NDP793.
Jean-Paul Sartre, Nausea. NDP82.
The Wall (Intimacy). NDP272.
P. D. Scott, Crossing Borders. NDP796.
Listening to the Candle. NDP747.
Delmore Schwartz, Selected Poems. NDP241.
In Dreams Begin Responsibilities. NDP454.
Hasan Shah, The Dancing Girl. NDP777.
C. H. Sisson, Selected Poems. NDP826.
Stevie Smith, Collected Poems. NDP562.
Novel on Yellow Paper. NDP778.
A Very Pleasant Evening. NDP804.
Gary Snyder, The Back Country. NDP249.
Turtle Island. NDP381.
Gustaf Sobin, Breaths' Burials. NDP781.
Muriel Spark, The Comforters. NDP796.
The Driver's Seat. NDP786.
The Public Image. NDP767.
Enid Starkie, Rimbaud. NDP254.
Stendhal, Three Italian Chronicles. NDP704.
Antonio Tabucchi, Pereira Declares. NDP848.
Nathaniel Tarn, Lyrics . . . Bride of God. NDP391.
Dylan Thomas, Adventures in Skin Trade. NDP183.
A Child's Christmas in Wales. NDP812.
Collected Poems 1934–1952. NDP316.
Collected Stories. NDP626.
Portrait of the Artist as a Young Dog. NDP51.
Quite Early One Morning. NDP90.
Under Milk Wood. NDP73.
Tian Wen: A Chinese Book of Origins. NDP624.
Uwe Timm, The Snake Tree. NDP686.
Lionel Trilling, E. M. Forster. NDP189.
Tu Fu, Selected Poems. NDP675.
N. Tucci, The Rain Came Last. NDP688.
Paul Valéry, Selected Writings.† NDP184.
Elio Vittorini, A Vittorini Omnibus. NDP366.
Rosmarie Waldrop, A Key into the Language of America.
NDP798.
Robert Penn Warren, At Heaven's Gate. NDP588.
Eliot Weinberger, Outside Stories. NDP751.
Nathanael West, Miss Lonelyhearts &
Day of the Locust. NDP125.
J. Wheelwright, Collected Poems. NDP544.
Tennessee Williams, Baby Doll. NDP714.
Cat on a Hot Tin Roof. NDP398.
Collected Stories. NDP784.
The Glass Menagerie. NDP218.
Hard Candy. NDP225.
A Lovely Sunday for Creve Coeur. NDP497.
The Roman Spring of Mrs. Stone. NDP770.
Something Cloudy, Something Clear. NDP829.
A Streetcar Named Desire. NDP501.
Sweet Bird of Youth. NDP409.
Twenty-Seven Wagons Full of Cotton. NDP217.
Vieux Carre. NDP482.
William Carlos Williams. Asphodel. NDP794.
The Autobiography. NDP223.
Collected Poems: Vol. I. NDP730.
Collected Poems: Vol. II. NDP731.
The Collected Stories. NDP817.
The Doctor Stories. NDP585.
Imaginations. NDP329.
In The American Grain. NDP53.
In The Money. NDP240.
Paterson. NDP806.
Pictures from Brueghel. NDP118.
Selected Poems (new ed.). NDP602.
Wisdom Books:
St. Francis. NDP477; Taoists. NDP509;
Wisdom of the Desert. NDP295.
Yūko Tsushima, The Shooting Gallery. NDP846.

For complete listing request free catalog from
New Directions, 80 Eighth Avenue, New York 10011   †Bilingual